THE BOY SCOUT
TRAIL BLAZERS

OR

SCOUTING FOR UNCLE SAM ON THE PIKE NATIONAL FOREST

BY

F. H. CHELEY

Author of "Buffalo Roost," "Told by the Campfire," etc.

ILLUSTRATED BY

CHARLES L. WRENN

PUBLISHED WITH THE APPROVAL OF
THE BOY SCOUTS OF AMERICA

PUBLISHERS
BARSE & CO.
NEW YORK, N. Y.   NEWARK, N. J.

THE NEW YORK
PUBLIC LIBRARY
154800B

E   1941   L

Copyright, 1917, by

Barse & Co.

The Boy Scout Trail Blazers

MADE IN U. S. A.

This scarce antiquarian book is included in our special *Legacy Reprint Series*. In the interest of creating a more extensive selection of rare historical book reprints, we have chosen to reproduce this title even though it may possibly have occasional imperfections such as missing and blurred pages, missing text, poor pictures, markings, dark backgrounds and other reproduction issues beyond our control. Because this work is culturally important, we have made it available as a part of our commitment to protecting, preserving and promoting the world's literature. Thank you for your understanding.

The little cavalcade swung into the trail that led to the
canyon road.   (*Page* 17.)   *Frontispiece.*

AFFECTIONATELY DEDICATED
TO EVERY
BOY SCOUT OF AMERICA
WHO HAS WON HIS
HONOR BADGE
FOR
FORESTRY

OCT 28 1940

TABLE OF CONTENTS

THE BOY SCOUT TRAIL BLAZERS

CHAPTER I

THE DEATH OF "FATHER TIME"

"I NEVER knew a fellow could have so much fun fishing," said Harry Carter to his Uncle Bob as they trudged along the narrow trail toward the old forester's cabin.

"Nor I either," chimed in the twin Scout. "It's trout for me every time after this. I'd rather have this little string of 'rainbows' than a whole wagonload of blue gills and perch. Fight? Oh, Jimminy, but they have spunk! The rest of the Troop will just laugh at us when we get to telling about this fishing trip."

"And like as not they will call every story we tell a 'whopper.' I wish we could have the whole bunch here for an outing. Wouldn't it be great sport to show them around!"

"And teach them to fish with a fly instead of just dangling a worm in the water. I'm going to

9

practice that fly casting stunt all winter, so when we come west again I can do as well as you do, Uncle,'' said Harry earnestly.

"Hurrah! there is the cabin just ahead," called Harry, joyfully, "and, believe me, I am the hungry kid. I'll do justice to Aunt's hot popovers and wild honey to-night, and sleep—oh, my!"

"We really ought to hear from Mother to-day, Harry," said Harvey thoughtfully. "My, but I do hate to think of going home next week. Why, ten days of this sort of life is just a teaser. I'd like to stay a whole year."

"So would I," affirmed Harry. "Say, Uncle Bob, wouldn't an eleven like the Supervisor or like Toney Carson make some of these college aggregations look pale around the gills? Talk about training—here's the place!"

"You're right, lad," said Mr. Standish in a pleased voice. "There is no place in the world where a fellow can grow so strong or train to endure so much as by living a clean, simple life out in the forest. These rangers are as hard as nails and scarcely, if ever, sick."

Aunt Belle was awaiting the little party and was very kind in her words of praise concerning the splendid catch of trout.

"I know you boys are just starved, and I have supper all ready. We'll fry those fish for breakfast. They will taste better to you then."

"Was there any mail?" asked Harry, almost eagerly.

"Not to-day," replied their aunt, "but there will be to-morrow, no doubt. You know it takes a long while for mail to get back here into the heart of the Rockies."

They were just at supper when—Br-r-r, Br-r-r —Br-r, went the telephone. Bob Standish rose from his chair and hastened to the receiver.

The call proved to be from Mr. Hastings, the District Supervisor of the forest.

"Go to Beaver Canyon to-morrow? Yes, I can go if you think best," said the forester. Then, after receiving careful orders of just what he was to do there, he hung up the receiver and returned to the table.

"I'm a bit disappointed, Scouts," he said to his two nephews. "However, orders are orders to a United States Forester and duty always comes before pleasure. We'll have plenty of time to tramp around and hunt when I get back. The Service has been having a great deal of trouble on the Reserve for some months with a gang of tie cutters. I hope you won't be too badly disappointed, but the Supervisor tells me that Old Luke, who is the leader of this notorious gang, is back on the range with his boys again. They have been cutting ties up Beaver Canyon, chopping anything and everything that takes their fancy, and I must go and make an investigation. You see, first of all it's against the law to cut any timber on a National Forest Reserve until it has been inspected and properly marked by one of the rangers; and then, too, it is especially dangerous to let these tie cutters go, because they not only waste choice trees to get out ordinary ties but they leave all the tops and limbs and chips just where the trees fall, and you realize, of course, that it is such carelessness that causes more than half of all the horrible fires that devastate our National Forests each year. Then, too—"

"But who is this Old Luke, Uncle?" interrupted Harry, who had become very interested in the story of the old tie cutter.

"Yes, do tell us about him, Uncle," added Harvey. "Is he a desperado?"

"You'd call him so in the city, boys, but out in these mountains we don't think of him just exactly that way. You see, the poor old duffer has had a hard time of it for a good many years. You boys, of course, do not know a great deal about the old sheep and cattle war. Some evening before you go back home I'll tell you all about it, but for now it was just this: the sheep raisers and the cattle growers all over these mountains grew to be bitter enemies, and there have been many pitched battles and much needless loss of life and much of bitter hatred. Now, Old Luke was first a cattle man and later a sheep man, and in the last big fight which took place up in the Big Basin, the cattle men cleaned Luke out—burned his corrals, butchered his sheep, and by accident shot his wife. Luke was left with two sturdy mountain lads, destitute. He took an oath, with his two boys, to avenge the death of their mother; consequently they have been the terror of certain sections for a half-dozen years. While the three of them are probably responsible for a half-dozen murdered cattle men in these parts, yet there has been no evidence.

"The Sheriff of Brown County finally offered a reward for Old Luke, dead or alive, and Luke disappeared. We heard nothing of him till two years ago, when Sheriff Brown's house and barns were mysteriously burned. Not many days later Old Luke was reported to have been seen up in a mining camp near Crystal Peak, but nothing came of it. Several times since, however, Luke and his two boys, now young men, have given the Forest Service a good deal of trouble by going into a choice woods and cutting, without any thought of the timber, hundreds of ties and drawing them out and selling them to the railroad. It is their way of making a living. Then to add to this Luke and the boys periodically get crazy drunk on 'rot-gut whisky.' It is at such times they cause all the rangers on the Reserve a good deal of uneasiness on account of the probability of fire starting in their crude camp. The Forestry Service have at last decided to rid themselves of this nuisance. The Supervisor is sending me after them. I must start very early in the morning.

"The Supervisor has had word that their tie camp is in a very dangerous condition with piles of dry slash and chips, and also that they have been stealing and butchering range cattle. He wants me to investigate the slash and to burn it if it looks too dangerous, and to bring Luke in with me if I can get him. It isn't a job I fancy very much, for Luke is a desperate character, but I am not afraid. I have talked with him many times about his troubles and he is just a poor, ignorant animal that lives by his wits. However, he is getting to be a real menace again and we must put a stop to it. His eldest son was a noted desperado in these hills a few years ago, but suddenly disappeared after a feud in a little mining town.

"A week ago the postmaster at Florence was robbed and shot, and as he was an old cow-man many people at once supposed the deed must have been done by a sheep-man. They suspect one of Luke's boys, but I think the whole story is a supposition. I don't believe either one of the boys knows enough to attempt any such an affair. At any rate the Supervisor thinks it will be best to keep our eyes open and for us to arrest Luke as a suspect if we can find him. I hate to go just at this time, but as I said, boys, orders are orders, and it will be but a two days' job.''

Both boys were disappointed and showed it plainly in spite of themselves.

"But, Uncle Bob," said Harry, coming to attention, his hand automatically coming to salute, "let us go with you, won't you? You know we are both First Class Scouts, and we could perhaps help you. Didn't you say that you might have to burn some of those slash piles on this trip?''

"Oh, do let us go!" chimed in Harvey. "I'm sure we could ride the extra horses, and we boys could make camp and cook for you. We have our camp kits and pocket axes with us, you know, and our blankets, and—''

"And I have my kodak, Uncle. I could photograph everything for you to illustrate your report with. I could develop the films right in camp with no trouble. Oh, do let us go! It would be such fun to illustrate a regular Government report for Uncle Sam.''

Mr. Standish looked down at the two stalwart lads and smiled.

"So you are First Class Scouts, are you, boys? Does that really mean that you are no longer Tenderfeet?'' Both boys nodded emphatically.

Even after an hour's talking and after every possible danger that might befall the lads had been carefully considered, the old ranger decided to think it over a bit longer, but with the result that it was finally agreed they should go. In two hours all three were busy making packs and getting their food bags together, for they must get away by breakfast if they were to make the trip in two days.

Mr. Standish was talking. "We will have to take 'Father Time' with us, boys, to carry our pack, for it will be hard traveling for the horses at best."

Both boys laughed heartily. "'Father Time'?" they cried together. "Why, Uncle, surely that donkey is too old to go on such a hard trip and carry this pack. It will weigh at least two hundred pounds."

"Don't worry, my lads, about that," chuckled the ranger. "'Father Time' has been carrying my pack for ten years and knows these hills like a book. We couldn't go without him. He and I are the best sort of friends, and more than once his 'horse sense' has saved me from making a very bad mistake. He is a very keen observer, too. I doubt if you could take him to any part of these mountains fifty miles away in any direction and lose him. He would invariably pick the shortest and best trail home. He's almost like having a camp mate. He stands lazily with his head in the smoke of my camp fire just as if he enjoys it, and he always eats all my left-overs. He is especially fond of pancakes and porridge."

Harvey laughed and laughed. "A donkey that is fond of pancakes and porridge! Say, Uncle, does he insist on having maple sirup on them, too?"

The first gray lights were just coming over Black Mountain when the little cavalcade swung into the trail that led to the canyon road—the boys eager, "Father Time" surprised, and Mr. Standish lost in thought about the mission he was starting on. He was worried over the fact that there might be a bit of gun play and— Yet they were Scouts, and if that organization had meant anything to them at all it had no doubt taught them to be self-reliant, resourceful, and to keep their head in an emergency. Ten to one, Luke was off in some mining camp anyway and that all they would really see of him would be his miserable wanton destruction of majestic pine and spruce and fir. He could see even then, in his mind's eye, the great heaps of topplings, the piles of fresh resinous chips, and the mounds of needles, dry as tinder and as inflammable as gun cotton. It was with no uncertain satisfaction that he realized that Luke and his gang of the cutters were at last about to be placed where they could do no more harm to the great swaying, breathing forest that Bob Standish had come to love as his very own.

Noon found them in the high hills by a stream of crystal water—melted snow, every drop of it, from the mighty glaciers on the sides of the Continental Divide. As Harvey built the fire, Harry began to open the various grub bags, selecting what they would need for their meal. Both scouts were so engrossed in proving to their uncle that they *could* prepare an appetizing meal that they paid little or no attention to their immediate surroundings. Ordinarily their keen eyes would have detected any unusual movements about them, but now they were so completely engrossed that they failed to even catch a glimpse of the tall, shambling tie cutter, who had twice circled their camp at a safe distance in order to be certain that he personally was not being hunted, for every tie cutter in the range was suspicious even of campers, and while the Forest Rangers were careful to not start trouble with them, they were never on friendly terms.

Uncle Bob led the horses down to the stream, then slipped the pack from "Father Time's" tired back, for the grades had been steep and they had pushed ahead hard all the morning. Soon the coffee pot was boiling merrily on a homemade tramel that Harry had deftly cut with his pocket ax. The flat stone that he had chosen to fry the venison on was already set and was heating, while the potatoes were put to boil in a convenient corner of the fire.

Harry, rising up suddenly from the fire to remove the coffee pot with a slender pot hook, bumped into a huge something that nearly knocked him off his feet and, to be perfectly honest, frightened him. Never before had so huge a head been thrust unceremoniously under his arm while he was getting dinner. He drew back with a gulp, only to behold the genial face of "Father Time." He laughed uproariously, and "Time," as if thoroughly understanding the whole situation, lay back one long ear and brayed.

"Oh, you Rocky Mountain canary!" laughed Harvey, as he brought a new armload of pine sticks for the fire.

"Three o'clock ought to see us in Beaver Canyon," said Mr. Standish, as the pack was again adjusted. "I want you boys to keep your eyes peeled for any signs of human life. These tie cutters have been persecuted so relentlessly all their lives that they are very hard to catch. We will be lucky if we even see them. We certainly won't see them if they see us first. Yet you can't tell when they are liable to take a pot-shot from same crag or tall tree. Last spring they shot Jake Town's old mare right out from under him.

He hunted for them three days but could not find them."

Late that afternoon they began to come to the first piles of toppings and chips. The possibility of being shot at from ambush kept all three as alert as squirrels. Even "Father Time" would prick up his long ears and look wise, suggesting that he had seen many strange things already that had escaped the eyes of the others.

The brush piles increased and here and there still lay a giant of the forest that had not as yet been sawed into lengths or dressed ready for tie timber. Finally the trail swung sharply to the left and revealed a tumbled-down, crude, make-shift shanty in the center of a devastated area. Everywhere lay the remnants of hundreds of great Engelmann Spruce.

The Ranger halted and carefully surveyed the scene before them. His heart was stirred with indignation. Suddenly he noted the thin column of smoke rising from the chimney. They must be at home. He ordered the boys to halt with the pack mule while he rode forward to investigate. When fifty feet from the shanty he called out a friendly "Halloo!" and waited. He got no response. He tried again with the same result. He glanced about him carefully for any signs of life. But for the tell-tale smoke, you might have thought the place had been deserted for months.

He rode to the door and knocked, but got no answer. He opened the door and peered in. There was no one at home, at least that he could see.

"Well, Scouts, they saw us first and are gone—for just how long, I don't know, but for the present we have this valley of destruction to ourselves. Let's pick a camp spot and set up our camp, for I see very plainly that unless they try to prevent us with their guns from some hidden shelter, we must burn a lot of this slash before we return. Harry, I'm so glad you brought that kodak. This evidence is conclusive. While the light is yet good I'll maneuver with you, in case some one might show up, and we'll get these pictures. Be careful with them and let's make every one count."

"Oh, I will," replied Harry with no little pride. "You know, Uncle, I have won my merit badge for photography."

The camp site was chosen at the edge of the clearing in an open spot away from the piles of slash. All hands set to, to make camp. First came the tent poles of aspen and the tent pins from forked sticks, and then the piles of sweet-scented pine boughs for the bed in the corner.

Harry and Uncle Bob took views all over the clearing and then came back to camp. After a little rest and more precautions against surprise, the Forester left the two boys while he strode off among the slash to chart and estimate the timber cut.   Over to one side of the clearing, and cleverly concealed under a generous pile of brush, he found nearly two hundred freshly hewn ties.   His indignation knew no bounds, and finally he strode over to the shanty again to make a better search.   He found that the fire had been hastily extinguished by pouring water in the stove, and furthermore he found that the ash pan had been freshly emptied.   He was an old woodsman of experience, and his curiosity was aroused as to where those ashes had been emptied.   He started on a search, and in a few moments, to his utter astonishment, he found where the hot ashes had been thrown into a slash pile to conceal them.   The only thing in the world that had saved a fire was the fact that it had rained heavily in the night, wetting the brush thoroughly, and that there had not been the slightest breath of wind since.   As he strode back towards the camp he was thinking of the labor and money it would take to re-forest so big an area.

Harry greeted him with shouts of enthusiasm.

"Oh, Uncle Bob, the pictures are simply great. Every one is a gem for detail and clearness.   I never made a sharper set of negatives."   He brought them and held them to the light for inspection.   Mr. Standish was pleased and complimented the lad on his work.

The evening meal was much enjoyed, for it had

been a strenuous day, and Uncle Bob was agreeably surprised at the art the boys had developed in camp-fire cooking. He could not have prepared a better supper himself, and if there was one thing he did pride himself upon it was upon his own ability to cook over an open fire.

"There is one thing above all others that the real forester must learn," he said, "and that is observation. After years of experience I can tell almost at a glance how many trees of a certain size there are to an acre in any given tract and how many feet of lumber in a tree. I can pick out a diseased or a beetle tree as far as I can see it. I can tell how old a tree is at a glance. I can make a map of any trail traveled during the day, and I can name every bird and tree and flower in the mountains."

"Why, Uncle Bob, you would make a good Boy Scout," cried Harvey enthusiastically. "Those are the things we are learning about all the time."

"I presume I would, boys," he laughed back. "If I understand this Scouting business at all, anyway, it is just a means to help you boys who are raised in the cities to live a normal, natural, useful life in an unnatural place. It's to help you retain the manly quality of the early pioneer and backwoodsman without giving up the bigger advantages of city life."

The evening passed quietly, and by eight-thirty

the fire was banked and the little party prepared to retire, for a strenuous day lay ahead. Harry gave the films their last bath in a pan of fresh water, and then carefully suspended them from the limbs of a near-by bush so they could not blow against anything until they should dry. In the morning they would begin to burn the huge slash piles. It was customary to wait until there was a good deal of snow to do it, for safety's sake, but this was an exception.

When Uncle Bob came in from picketing the horses "Father Time" followed him to the fire and there eagerly devoured the pan of scraps that had been saved for him. The last recollections that Harry had before he fell asleep was of old "Father Time" standing above the fire, his long ears forward, his shaggy old head dropped to a comfortable angle, and his occasional grunt as he breathed the smoke-scented air.

When the boys awoke in the morning, Uncle Bob already had the fire burning and was busily engaged in making sketches and figures in his note book. The boys emerged together, their hair towsled and their legs stiff from the ride. Uncle Bob looked up and called a kindly "Good Morning," then turning to Harvey he said:

"Harvey, I wish you would slip on your boots and look about for 'Father Time.' He is gone. I never before knew him to leave the campfire, but he's gone as sure as fate. The horses are scattered and I think some of these tie cutters have been about."

Harvey was off in a flash. Surely a Scout that could follow tracks and play stalking in the woods would have no trouble to locate so large an animal as "Father Time."

Harry made a dive for his films, and, to his utter astonishment, they were gone, too. He looked about him in surprise, and then supposing his uncle had taken them down he returned and asked about them.

"Why, I didn't touch them, my lad," he replied. "Are they gone, too?"

Gone they were, and no trace of them whatever was left on the bushes where they had hung.

"Hum!" said Mr. Standish. "Mule gone, pictures gone. I don't think Luke has brains enough to do a trick like that, but I'm not so sure about the boys. I've heard they are nobody's fools. The mule was our only pack animal. We can't carry our camp material without him. The pictures certainly will condemn any tie cutter, for a camera doesn't lie. I see it all, my boy. This is their game. What a fool I am! They have stolen the pictures. They probably reasoned you used up all your films, and by taking the mule they figured we would either have to leave our equipment, which they would promptly appropriate, or that we would be delayed long enough so that they and the old man could get safely out of the country before we could get back and make our report. Well, it's too bad, my boy, too bad.''

Just then Harvey came tearing through the woods from the direction of the stream.

''I found him, Uncle; I found him—but he's dead!''

''Dead?'' echoed the Ranger, as he rose and grabbed his gun. ''Where, lad?''

Harvey led the way to where ''Father Time'' lay dead in the grass. Mr. Standish made a hasty examination, a puzzled look on his face. ''This Scout cooking doesn't seem to have agreed with you, old boy,'' he said sadly. ''And not even a shovel to give you a decent burial! But we'll not leave you for the birds—we'll cremate you. The point just now is, what killed you? Could Luke have done it? It doesn't seem possible, and yet—''

Breakfast was eaten in silence, and then the Ranger told the boys to break and pack camp and to arrange to take with them just what they must have, for what they did take would have to be tied on behind their saddles. While they were busy at this job Mr. Standish went to see what could be done with the body of their faithful friend.

As he stood looking at the dead animal he had

an idea. Hurriedly he walked to the trees where
the films had hung and carefully examined the
nearby brush and the ground. There were unmistakable prints of "Father Time's" feet, and
to one side and a few feet away lay the sticks that
had been attached to the bottom of the films to
keep them from curling. "Father Time" had
eaten the precious negatives and they had killed
him.

Uncle Bob carried the sticks to camp and offered his explanation. The boys listened in
amazement. Then turning, Harry said, half
sadly:

"Harvey, I don't know anything about scouting when there is a mule in the party, do you?"

"Anyway, the old boy took some mighty vivid
impressions of this tie cutter's camp with him,"
laughed Harvey.

An hour later, just as they were preparing to
start home, the strangest procession the boys had
ever seen came out of the woods opposite their
camp and halted. There was an old, old man—
gray-bearded and stoop-shouldered, and two illy
clad, dirty younger men. Each one had his hands
securely lashed to his side and sat astride a cow
pony. Just behind them were two well-mounted
cowboys, a heavy six shooter on each hip. They
halted and Mr. Standish went out to meet them.

"Guess these be the scamps you have been

after for a long spell, Mr. Standish,'' volunteered one of the cowboys. "We rounded them up for you, but had an awful scrap before we collared them. Guess Jim Temple will be laid up the rest of his days, but we proposed to settle this tie cutting gang this time once for all. We're going to take them direct to the Supervisor. If he don't jug 'em tight we are going to have a hangin' bee over in Skunk Canyon, 'cause we just naturally can't stand this here pesky thievin' any longer. What's more, a man's life isn't safe with this gang of desperadoes running the country. I tell you it's time to act serious.''

"Four calves in three weeks, to say nothing of the ornerist fire we have ever had to fight,'' growled the other cowboy. "It's got to stop. Just take a look at the valley too. Suppose you were here to get 'em, wasn't you?''

The prisoners glowered fiercely at the men and cursed as the Ranger carefully examined the ropes that bound them, for he realized that he was dealing with desperate characters and meant to take no chances. He had evidence aplenty, and now he had Old Luke and the boys and was ready to return.

"I believe we have all of the gang right here,'' he said, "and the Supervisor will be very grateful to you men for your help.''

"Seems to me there is another one yet,'' said

the first cowboy, "but we couldn't find him—at least there have been four of them mixed up in some of these raids, but we'll get him if he shows up, and we'll put him with the rest."

Harry, who was watching Old Luke, noted that as the cowboy spoke, Luke winked to the oldest boy and nodded his head knowingly.

CHAPTER II

MR. STANDISH force-marched the little party of tie cutters down the canyon, but in order to avoid any commotion he took them over a little used trail direct to the home of the Sheriff, sending the boys to the cabin ahead of him.

Aunt Belle had expected them and had a generous hot supper all prepared.

"Was there any mail?" cried both boys, as they entered the gate.

"Yes," answered Mrs. Standish. "one for each of you."

"Was mine from Mother, Aunt Belle?" insisted Harvey, "or from the Scout Master? It's about time he was writing us, it seems to me. Why, the Troop has had time to go all to smash in the week we have been gone, and no word. He promised to write. I'm wondering how Prell is making it as Patrol Leader in my absence."

Under Harry's plate was a big fat letter from Mother and under Harvey's one from the Scout Master.

"Well, what do you know about that!"

30

ejaculated Harry at length, ripping his open and scanning the page hurriedly.

"Well, I'll be jiggered," echoed Harvey, hastily re-reading to make sure he had made no mistake. "Scarlet fever epidemic!—Epidemic, that means everybody has it. Why say, Aunt Belle, just look at this. And we aren't to go home."

"Prell has it, and Smith, and Dobson from our Troop," cried Harry, "and Mr. Tate is quite sick. Can't go home! Why not, Harvey?"

"Why, Mother says it isn't safe for us to come. School isn't to open, and no one can leave or enter the town. Here, read it yourself. Let's see what Mr. Tate has to say."

The boys hastily exchanged letters and began again. Both faces brightened at the same second as one shouted:

"Uncle Bob, we don't have to go home and we are to stay with you indefinitely—that might mean forever. Say, isn't that bully? I'm sorry for the other fellows, but that's great for us— no school, no work; just hike and fish and—"

"Hear stories and eat popovers and sleep and read," interrupted the other lad. But Uncle Bob was busy reading the letter that had come to him also from the boys' mother, and had nothing to say. At last he laid it down and thought meditatively for a full moment.

"Well, boys, we'll be glad to have you with us,

as far as that goes, but listen to me—you can't stay here with me all Fall and just loaf away your time. That's contrary to all principles of conservation, and you know that that is my hobby. No, if you are going to stay with me, you just make up your minds you are going to school just the same, and to the most practical school teacher in all the world—Old Dame Nature, in her big school-house of 'Out-doors.' You'll get to hike, and fish, and all that, all right, but you will be responsible for definite tasks and be expected to learn your lessons just the same. What's more, remember, I'm to be the School Principal, and I'll see to it that there is no loafing. Just yesterday the Supervisor was wishing for more forest guards so some of the rest of us could give our undivided attention to the beetle pest that is raging just now on upper Rock Creek; besides, many tie cutters are making no end of extra work just now. Seems that every day brings news of some trouble of their making. I will make forest rangers out of you lads, and we'll mighty soon tell if there is any good in this Boy Scout business. I'll talk it over with Mr. Hastings at once." He rose and went to the telephone.

The boys fairly hugged themselves with delight —real forest rangers on the biggest of all Uncle Sam's Reserves! "I'm going to start a diary at once," cried Harry, "and call it 'Scouting for Uncle Sam on the Pike National Forest.'"

"I'm going to call mine the 'Adventures of a Tenderfoot,'" said Harvey, "and by keeping careful notes we can have a lot of worth-while information for the Troop when we do get back."

"And what's more, we'll both get busy and win our merit badges for forestry," said Harry. "We are lucky dogs for sure. But remember we have simply got to make good in this undertaking, for the honor of Plainville Troop."

The Supervisor was entirely willing to try the scheme as long as the boys were under Mr. Standish's direct charge, so all details were left to him. The rest of the evening was spent in working out plans. The Standish cabin was to become headquarters for all three Foresters. Harry was to be given the Goose-trail that led to the top of Black Mountain for his special territory, and Harvey was to take the Bowlder-trail that led to "Little Big Chief." That would be his last lookout. Tompkins, who had been riding these two trails, alternate days, would thus be freed to work with Mr. Standish and the Supervisor on the beetle ravishes of upper Beaver Canyon.

"I'll expect each of you to carry a note book, boys," Uncle Bob declared, "and I want you to make careful notes of everything—such as kinds of trees, weather signs, plant and animal life, tracks, and so forth; then, evenings that I get home, we will have a little school together and see what we can learn. I must find out what good observers you are first of all, for no matter how much training you have along other lines, if you are not good observers you will never make good foresters. I'll ride both trails with you to-morrow and explain your duties carefully so there will be no mistaking them. I am about to give each of you boys a tremendous responsibility. You are to become the sole guardians of a half-million acres of splendid forest, and one careless hour and the honor of our station is gone. If your Scouting has been thorough it will stand you in good stead. I will supply you each with a pair of field glasses and a gun. For the present we will have to get along with what horses we have, but that can be arranged. We will have a thirty minutes' target practice each morning before breakfast—not because you will need to kill anything but because it will train you eye and hand to harmonious action and give you keener judgment. Remember that while I am your uncle, during working hours I am your supervisor in the service and I will expect you to act accordingly.''

Each boy wrote an enthusiastic letter home that night and then retired, for they were weary from

the long excitement of capturing Old Luke, and
from the trip into the timber; besides, on the
morrow they were to become assistants to Uncle
Sam and must be in the pink of condition.

Uncle Bob and Aunt Belle sat a long time by the
fire planning, Uncle Bob chuckling all the while.
He had always had his pet theories of how boys
ought to be schooled, but had never been fortu-
nate enough to be the father of a boy, so all his
ideas had gone to waste until now.

"I'll give those lads the best year's schooling
of their lives, Belle," he said, between chuckles.
"Mary will never know them when she gets them
back home again. I'm not much on the Algebra
and Latin, I know, but I can teach them a heap of
things that aren't in books."

The sun was just peeping over the crag-crowned
summit of Cheyenne as the new recruits rode out
of the corral and into the wide trail that led into
the heavy timber. There was a fresh bracing
quality to the air that fairly sent the blood tin-
gling through the boys' veins.

"There's a yellow pine and there's an Engelmann spruce and a quaking aspen and a silver
spruce," called Harry in high spirits.

"And they are all ours, Harry," said Harvey
half seriously. "I suppose we will come to know
them all just like we do the boys—their good
points and the weak ones, what they are good for

and what they are liable to do under given circumstances.''

"Yes, and who knows but that we will be called on to bandage some of them or to amputate a limb or a finger. 'First aid' to trees—ha! ha! There is one thing certain, though, we won't have to give them any artificial respiration. The bandaging part will be easy.''

"See those woodpeckers!'' cried Harry, excitedly. "Why, there must be twenty of them on that one tree—'Red Heads' we call them. Uncle, what are they doing there together?''

Uncle Bob laughed. "Why, boys, that is Dr. Flicker's laboratory of surgery.''

"Of surgery?'' questioned Harry.

"Yes, we would not have a decent standing forest in America to-day if it wasn't for the faithful, untiring efforts of all the Doctor Woodpeckers. They are the forest tree surgeons. They annually consume millions upon millions of insects that devour the trees. There, just take your glass and watch that fellow there. See how he taps and taps upon the trunk. His keen sense of hearing tells him when he has found the hollowed-out nest of a worm or insect and he sets to work at once to dig him out. He does it so cleverly and so neatly that in most instances the tree heals over again and gets well. Just imagine a million such birds operating here in our forest, eating perhaps two hundred worms or insects a day. Don't you see? I'll tell you more about old Dr. Woodpecker some other time. Harry, here is your first lookout. Let's dismount.''

In a moment all three were standing on a rugged cliff that looked far out over the whole of Beaver Canyon to Cheyenne, while above them and behind them were the tops of a million trees.

''In case you are able to distinguish a fire from any of these lookouts, pause long enough to carefully get the exact lay of the land, deliberately choose your path as nearly as is possible, and then make all haste to the scene of trouble. If you are on the alert, it isn't probable that a fire will get enough of a start but that prompt, heroic action on your part will put it out. However, if you should see that it is already a heavy fire, ride to the cabin, ring the Supervisor on the 'phone and give him detailed directions; then go at once to the fire yourself and use your judgment about attacking it. Stay until help comes, and if none comes stay yourself until all has been done that is possible. Keep a sharp lookout for campers, and in case any cross your track be friendly to them, but in the course of your conversation warn them to be very cautious, as they are the most dangerous of all causes of forest fires.

''Yonder you see a big fire-burned area. You can tell it by the small, dense second growth that is coming on. Evidently the wind was blowing due south and a gale, as there is a fairly straight boundary on both sides. The river shut off the ground-fire on the left and the draught of the canyon held it from burning too high on the ridge. It was probably started by lightning, for that is what we call 'Spike Peak Canyon.' Do you notice how many of those Western yellow pines have a dead top? Well, those are the result of lightning. We are removing them from the Reserve as fast as possible, for it is in just such wounded trees as those that all sorts of insect-pests, including the beetle, germinate and multiply by the millions. Rarely, if ever, will an insect attack a perfectly healthy tree. It's a good deal like disease, boys. It rarely can find a footing in a perfectly sound, healthy body."

They were mounted again when a sudden shrill squeal of pain in an adjoining thicket, punctuated by a hoarser growl of anger and despair, attracted them. In a second Uncle Bob was on the ground again, his big Colt revolver gleaming in his hand. Before the boys could slip out of their saddles Mr. Standish had slipped into the thick young spruce. The boys pushed in after him. The squealing increased and the growling became a roar of rage. Soon they caught sight of Uncle Bob just ahead, with the bushes parted, gazing down into a hidden gulch. He motioned them to come quietly, while he whispered, "It's old 'Bald Spot' and her cubs, and they are in an awful calamity."

The boys crouched law and gazed in the direction of the wild pandemonium, surprised at Uncle Bob's chuckle and his unconcern. Surely, if there was a whole valley full of angry bears, it was no time to be laughing. But laugh Uncle Bob did in loud guffaws. The boys had never seen such a curious sight before. Below them lay a recently blown-down spike top that had been broken in two about half way up by the terrific fall. To one side sat an old black bear on her haunches, pawing her nose and head as if all the mosquitoes in Alaska had suddenly settled upon her smelling apparatus, while tumbling on the ground about her were three half-grown cubs, going through more strange antics than the Scouts ever dreamed a bear was capable of. They were more agile than a cat and quicker than lightning.

The Scouts instinctively turned to Mr. Standish, who was now convulsed with laughter, for an explanation.

"Honey," he managed to say—"wild honey. They have been robbing a bees' hive in that fallen tree and the whole swarm is upon them."

Suddenly the mother bear broke and ran for the

timber, pawing wildly as she went, the cubs after her in full retreat. As they turned to go to their horses Harry stopped and listened.

"I thought I heard some one walking over by the horses," he said, "but I must have been mistaken for I don't see any one."

"That's one of the tricks of the forest," said Mr. Standish. "You often think there is some one near you. Keep your eyes open always and take a good look at every stranger. Many suppose that the robber of the Florence Post Office is hiding in this valley, but I don't think it probable or we would have seen something of him."

They were mounted again now and soon rounded a mighty monolith of pink granite, then began to descend in long, graceful curves through the trees. In a few moments they were in "Spike Top" Canyon by a majestic water fall.

"The first time I came to these falls, boys, I shot an immense twelve-point buck just there, but it was only because we were badly in need of meat. I never come to them now but I imagine that I see the princely fellow lift his head from the cool stream and gaze at me pleadingly. What wouldn't I have given after it was over to have been able to bring him back to life again, for I have learned since that killing the wild things in the forest is like pulling the flowers from your garden."

By noon they had returned to the cabin, and ate ravenously, but were eager to be off again on the other trail. Just before leaving, the Supervisor 'phoned Mr. Standish that a strange man had been reported seen wandering in the valley and that, in all probability, it was the Florence robber; every man in the Service was being informed, and a sharp lookout was to be kept by all.

"Yonder is a beaver dam," said Uncle Bob, early in the afternoon, and both boys were all interest in a moment, for they were both members of the Beaver Patrol and had had carefully drilled into them many times the admirable qualities of Mr. Beaver, from his industry to his foresight.

"Have you ever really seen them at work, Uncle Bob?" asked Harry, eagerly. "I'd give a great deal to see a real beaver doing something."

"Oh, yes, many a time, boys. I could spin you yarns all night about them if I once got started. They are, in a way, pets of mine, for you see they are the real engineers of the forests—conservation experts, every one of them. Every fertile valley in these Rocky Mountains is the result of beaver. Every mountain meadow owes its existence to them. They regulate the flow of rivers, they build ponds that act as settlers to catch the rich sediment that is washed from the mountainsides in the spring, and when these crude ponds fill, they courageously build new dams to back the water up farther. Once, over in the Rock Creek Canyon after a terrific cloudburst that washed out hundreds of beaver dams and eroded the fertile meadows to a depth of twenty feet, I discovered the remains of eight beaver dams built one upon another, showing that there was twenty feet of rich leaf-mold and sediment settled upon an otherwise rocky gulch. Seeds had found lodgment and grew rapidly—first an aspen grove, then an alder thicket, and then young spruce, and now, a splendid forest. Many of the finest lodge pole pine on the Pike Forest are in that canyon growing in that great depth of fertile soil gathered by beaver dams.

"Those crude, dome-shaped piles of mud and sticks are their homes, and in them, in the winter, they pile their store of tender aspen poles that serve as food and later as material for their dams. Sometimes I have seen twenty beaver at one time all working together. To 'work like a beaver' is to work indeed, and to do it with little fuss and noise. No boss is needed.

"Once I saw—" Two shots rang out on the still, clear air and resounded up the valley. Uncle Bob stopped short.

"That is my signal to return to the cabin without delay," he said. "I wonder what's up—convict found? More trouble at that saw mill, I'll

just bet. I'll be so glad when we get these spike
tops all cut out and that saw mill gone. They
worry me almost to death. First, it's a few of
my chickens gone, then a horse for a few days,
then a drunken fight among the cutters, in which
some one gets killed. See here, boys, I am going
to take the short cut home and let you follow the
trail on in, so you can see just exactly how it comes
out on the mountain. You ought to reach the
cabin by five, if you keep moving. Remember,
keep your eyes open. Be prepared. Good-by."
He was gone at a lively gallop, and the two boys
found themselves alone in a strange canyon with
many miles of trail ahead of them to be traveled
before night.

"I'm certainly interested in these beaver,
Harry, and I'd be tickled to death to see just one,"
said Harvey. "Let's see, wasn't it from that big
crag that he said he had watched them so often?
Then our trail must go that way. Let's hurry on
and perhaps it will be our good luck to see one
to-day."

A few moments' riding brought them at last to
the big overhanging cliff, and slipping quickly
from their horses they hurried to the edge, carefully parted the bushes and gazed down into the
placid pond below them with its ragged dam
across one end. Breathlessly they waited, their
eyes riveted on the pond, but there was scarcely a

ripple on its glassy surface. They thought they were doomed to disappointment and were about to retreat to their horses when Harry nudged Harvey gently and pointed his finger. "See there!" he cried. A lone beaver had risen quietly to the surface of the water, just in front of the largest mud hut, and was noiselessly making for the aspen park, swimming with the utmost ease through the majestic inverted shadows of pine and crag. Suddenly he stopped, raised his head higher as if he scented danger, and then making a complete circuit of the pond came back to the aspen park and climbed onto the bank, just as a man stepped out of the bushes and then disappeared in the timber. Soon two other beaver clambered out and awkwardly made their way to the aspen grove, apparently intent on something. Both boys had their glasses out now and were soon entirely engrossed in the movements of the little engineers, completely forgetting the man they had seen for that fleeting instant. Each beaver selected an aspen and after a brief study of it went to work to cut it down.

"You don't think that big one will try to cut that huge aspen, do you?" breathed Harry.

"What can they want with that big tree, anyway?" said Harvey. "Surely, it's too tough for food."

"Look! Look!— Isn't that splendid?" exclaimed Harry. "If he succeeds in cutting it, it will fall exactly across the dam and will make an excellent network to build to, and perhaps he will save the smaller branches for food."

Evidently Mr. Beaver was satisfied with his calculations, for quite as suddenly as he had come he put his forepaws against the yellow trunk, spread his hind legs, braced himself, sat back on his broad paddle-like tail, and calmly began to chisel away the bark at a convenient height from the ground and on the side of the tree away from the dam. The boys were fairly amazed at the progress he made and at the deft way in which he used the long chisel teeth that were set in the extreme front of his jaw. Shortly there was a strange thumping on the ground, and both boys turned just in time to see a three-inch aspen topple and fall. The ax-man had given the signal by whacking his tail three times on the soft ground beneath him.

So entirely engrossed were the boys that they had entirely forgotten that they were Forest Rangers on guard or that they had ever had such things as horses. As they sat thus, with their backs to the trail, gazing into the pond below, suddenly the same gaunt, ragged man they had seen below them emerged from the trail and calmly stood watching them. His face was covered with a long growth of dirty whiskers, his clothes were torn and ragged, and his head and shoulders drooped noticeably. He cast furtive glances about him, as if to determine if he were pursued, and was about to cross over to the boys when his eye caught sight of the two horses. Suddenly he became as alert as a cat. Hurrying to where they were grazing he hastily tied one to a nearby branch, slipped into the saddle of the other, then carefully guiding the horse off the hard trail onto the soft pine needles, was gone. Ten minutes afterward the boys heard loud voices coming up the trail, and in a moment were on their feet and hurrying to their horses.

"It's Uncle Bob," breathed Harry.

"And the Supervisor, and Tompkins," added Harvey. "And—gracious, it's getting dusk! We are in for it now, I'll bet. Why, we ought to have been home by now. What shall we do—wait for them, or go on? Do you suppose they are looking for us?"

There was a spirited gallop, and the men emerged from the timber. To the boys' utter astonishment, all were heavily armed, sober faced, and excited.

"Where's my horse?" cried Harry, in consternation.

"Who tied mine this way? I'm sure I didn't," said Harvey.

"Hello, boys!" cried Uncle Bob. "Gracious,

I'm glad you are safe! Have you seen any one pass you on this trail the last two hours? What has kept you here so long, anyway? Where is your horse, Harry?''

The boys explained what they had been doing, but were at a total loss to account for the missing horse or for the other horse being tied. Evidently they had had a visitor.

"He came this way, Bob," said the Supervisor, positively, "and he is at this hour racing for freedom on a Forest Service horse. That is very unfortunate. If he hadn't come onto these green Rangers we would have had him by night, for he was about exhausted." Then, turning disgustedly, he said, "Boys, I thought you were Scouts. I believe a herd of elephants could cross your trail in plain daylight and you wouldn't know it."

"Who came this way, Uncle Bob?" asked both boys eagerly. "Oh, we are so sorry if we were careless. We know we are green, but you told us to keep our eyes open for wild life and—''

"The real 'wild life' got by you boys this time," said Uncle Bob, kindly. "A real, sure-enough desperado crossed your trail during the last hour, and we were so in hopes you boys, being seasoned Scouts, would detain him or trail him until we could come to your help. The entire county is hunting him just now with armed posses. He is not many miles from this pond, either. But, even with the horse, he has no means to make fire and we will starve him out yet. He has been on the constant move for forty-eight hours, and must soon be exhausted.''

"But, Uncle," called Harry in great excitement, "my haversack with my lunch and scout-ax and matches were on the saddle. I hung it there while we went to watch the beaver. I'll bet we saw your man, though."

The Supervisor scowled again and muttered something more about "greenhorns" as he swung his pony about in the trail, impatient to be off. Uncle Bob only whistled his consternation, and then, as if to make the very best of a bad job, he ordered the boys to at once start for the cabin with all possible speed.

"I'll go ahead. The scoundrel might go to the cabin, and if by any chance he should get hold of a weapon his final capture will be expensive. But get him we must, and I had counted on you boys."

"I'm sure he won't get any weapon with Aunt Belle there," said Harvey, quite positively.

A half hour later the main trail crossed an abandoned trail that in former years had led to the cabin. As the boys approached, Harry thought he heard a horse whinny. He stopped, dropped into the bushes and waited. Harvey was hardly out of sight on his horse when the young spruce divided and the desperado, mounted on

Harry's pony, came down the other trail. Over his shoulder was slung a sawed-off Winchester rifle that Harry suddenly realized belonged to Uncle Bob. The Scout groaned to himself as he thought of all the possible consequences of their little carelessness.

"Hum! We haven't honored Plainville Troop much to-day," he said, as the horse and rider disappeared down the trail. "Well, by Jimminy, I've learned my lesson, and I'll show that Supervisor yet." The boy was speeding down the trail now, and his mind was busy.

CHAPTER III

"A DESPERADO, a sawed-off Winchester, a cook kit, ax, pony, and supplies —that's going some!" cried the Supervisor, "and a dozen of us hunting him ready to shoot him on sight. If he hadn't gotten that horse we would have had him."

"Easy a bit, Mr. Hastings," said Bob softly. "That won't get us anywhere now. Let's do less talking and some real thinking. It strikes me that whoever that chap was, he knows this valley like a book. Do you suppose he could be one of those discharged cutters? How did he know Belle was gone? You don't suppose there could be any connection between that rascal and Belle's disappearance, do you?"

Pandemonium reigned at the Forester's cabin. Uncle Bob was noticeably excited, while the Supervisor was almost beside himself with rage. Aunt Belle was gone and had left no word of any kind. Mr. Standish's sawed-off Winchester was also gone, and a whole box of ammunition. The larder had also been raided, but so far as everything else was concerned it seemed to be in its usual place.

"I supposed it was Belle who gave me the signal to come to the cabin," said Mr. Standish. "If I hadn't met you, Tompkins, coming on the trail and gotten information of the affair at Florence, I, of course, would have gone straight to her to see what was wrong. She often leaves this way when some one summons her to some lonely ranch where there is sickness, but she always leaves a note, in case I might come home and find her gone. I can't understand it."

"She might have gone to the sawmill, Bob," suggested Tompkins, "expecting to get back before supper. They are always needing a nurse over there anyway. I'll just hop on Nance and ride over that way."

The boys hurried in and found the two men facing each other in the center of the kitchen, each trying to find an answer in the face of the other.

"I saw him, Uncle Bob," cried Harry, between breaths, "and he had a gun—a funny, pug-nosed one. He had a basket on his arm, too, and he was smiling. It was the same man we saw yesterday in Spike Top and again at the Beaver Dam."

Both men gazed at the boy as if they had not heard aright.

"He was going due North on a cow trail," continued Harry, "and rode as easily as if he had been born in the saddle. He didn't see me, though, for I was hidden in the bushes. I heard the pony whinny, and I hid. I'd know him again in a thousand. He was tall, and his eyes were small and very sharp, and his ears were very large. He was awfully humped over and—''

The gate clicked and all jumped to the window to see what was coming. Aunt Belle and Tompkins were hurrying toward them, talking rapidly.

"Oh, Bob! What has happened?" she cried, as she opened the door. "I have been such a fool. I should have known better, but he was so earnest and I didn't think, but just hurried. He said that a cutter had cut an artery just above the knee, and that I must go at once. He was riding on over to Duffields to telegraph for the doctor. I just took my little emergency kit and hurried as fast as I could go. At the mill they told me I had been misinformed, that there had been no accident at all, and told me about half of the cutters being off hunting a man that has escaped an armed posse at Florence,—first, he robbed the post office at that place and then fatally shot the Post Master. A rumor has reached the mill that it was High Tucker, a former boss cutter. The Sheriff believed he would head straight for this county, hoping to find shelter in one of the lumber camps.''

At the name of High Tucker, Tompkins' eyes

suddenly snapped, and then he turned quickly away.

"What sort of a looking fellow came to the door and told you of the accident, Belle?" asked Bob, eagerly.

"Very tall, with dirty whiskers, keen blue eyes, and a sad sort of a face."

"That was him, Aunt Belle!" cried Harry, in great excitement. "Exactly!"

"Well, he is riding at large, with my shot gun, shells, and horse," said Mr. Standish, "to say nothing of your to-day's baking, and dear knows what else."

"High Tucker, eh?" said the Supervisor. "I don't believe it. He was a harmless half-wit, and some one is trying to put a game on him. When he worked on the range with us he used to keep referring to the days when he was a real bad man, but we always thought it was just in his mind."

"But no one is sure it was High. It might be some one else. High was always so good to folks in trouble," said Mrs. Standish.

"Well, I would know High if I should see him, anyway," said Bob. "High and I are old friends. If I thought it was him, I'd hate to hunt him like a deer. He is a poor, harmless fellow who would do no one any wrong. There must be some mistake on this business."

"High was the best man on a beetle hunt that I have ever seen," said the Supervisor. "I'd like to have him now for a few weeks, until we get those trees cut and burned. They are spreading every day, and thousands upon thousands of acres of excellent forest are going to be infected there in another month. He could go out and find the mother-beetle tree in an endless tract, after experienced foresters had spent weeks trying to locate the source of infection. If he would just leave that 'rot-gut' whisky alone I could give him employment and decent quarters all the time; but he loves life in some lonely gulch too well to live with other folks."

After supper, as they sat about talking over the events of the day, Tompkins suddenly changed the subject.

"Well, what are we going to do about it tomorrow?" he enquired. "Are we going to give up that bug expedition and hunt poor High, or are we going to get at that beetle attack? Seems to me that is of a heap more importance just now than capturing High. I'd hate to see the old fellow hung, anyway. I don't believe now, and never will, that it was High. Sounds a lot more like one of the tricks of Old Luke's boys."

"You are right, Tompkins," said the Supervisor. "It's now or never on that beetle deal. We must be at it to-morrow. I have no time to be hunting High Tucker. I had about decided to take these greenhorn Scouts along with us, to help care for camp, so we could give our whole time to the pest, but I don't know. I'm afraid they would be off chasing sunbeams somewhere. How about it, Bob?"

Both boys were eager, even if they were hurt just a little, and were crazy to prove their real worth to the skeptical Supervisor. It was now in this trying moment that their Scoutcraft won the day. Both boys were sorely tempted to speak up and give him a piece of their minds for rubbing it in so often, yet they remembered that he was their superior in the Service and that a Scout is always courteous.

"Sir, give us a chance. You are judging us too quickly. I doubt if you would (he was about to say—'have seen that outlaw yourself if you had been in our place to-day,' but a sharp nudge from Harry brought him back to himself, and he continued, a bit confused) find better camp builders, even among your trained rangers, than we boys. Give us but a chance."

"How about it, Bob?" questioned Mr. Hastings.

"Well, I'd hate to leave them here just now, with a desperado roaming these hills armed with my old rifle. I believe in the lads, sir, but will agree to whatever you say. They were a great help to me on my little trip after the tie cutters, and can certainly cook on an open fire. Old Barnabas Day is not in it with these lads when it comes to handling a skillet, I tell you that; and I'd feel better to take them along with me, under the circumstances, if they can go with your approval."

"Go, they shall," said the Supervisor, positively, "and we'll see about their cooking. I'll bet they can't either of them toss flap-jacks or make a decent twist, but they will do to fetch water and such things." Harry saw a twinkle in the gray eyes for the first time, and felt ever so much more comfortable.

"If we are to go, sir, tell us a bit about these beetle pests, won't you, so we can understand what you are all talking about."

"Well said, my lad. That is the proper attitude. We don't any of us know any too much about the ravagers, but such expeditions as this we are about to start on are constantly adding new information. Every species of tree in America, save the Giant Sequyas of California, is subject to terrific onslaughts of insects that take an annual toll in loss to the forest of many million dollars. In fact, so great are the depredations of the beetles and weevils that it is now a well established fact that they cause more loss to timber each year than all the forest fires combined. There are thousands of insects that prey on trees from the time they are a seedling to ripe old age, attacking roots, bark, tender shoots, stems, blossoms, and fruit.

"The pine beetle burrows into the trees to lay its eggs in the tender inner bark. When once inside they cut transverse tunnels about the trees and in a short time completely girdle it, cutting off its supply of sap. The tree quickly dies, and soon becomes the nesting place of countless millions of little grubs that finally hatch into beetles again, and the whole family of, say a half million, swarm out and attack the trees nearest to them. Stunted trees, spike tops, and partially dead timber are the best breeding places until the swarm becomes large enough, then they attack everything in sight, and not uncommonly deforest a vast area in one season. Now, of course, the birds prey on these beetles, and certain species of wasps are very fond of the grubs when they can be gotten at. The woodpecker is especially valuable for his services in this connection, and if we just had enough of them that we could transport from place to place, as a pest makes itself known, we would soon get it under control, provided we could locate the infected spots before the swarm becomes too large.

"Old High Tucker could locate the infected trees from their color, just as far as he could see them, and I wish that we had him to help us now, instead of hunting him for murder. The most efficacious way to fight them is to cut the trees while the grubs are in process of incubation and burn them, thus destroying millions of the little demons before their appetite for fresh bark has matured. It is arduous labor, but there is a certain satisfaction in it.

"There is another way that works very satisfactorily for certain species, and it is as simple as it is efficacious. We choose a large spruce, completely girdle it with an ax, and let it die. The beetles for miles away seem to be able to smell the chemical change, and come by the thousands to bury themselves in the sweet resinous bark. At the proper time the tree is then cut and burned. We shall probably use both methods on this trip. Now, if you lads are to accompany us, Tompkins and I must ride down to my cabin yet to-night and get a couple of extra horses. Gracious—nine o'clock! We must be away. We will be back at sunrise and will have horses for you. Better leave that other pony for Old High if he should come in our absence. Now, away to bed, all of you."

The boys had been in bed several hours when they were rudely awakened by a loud whinny and a rattle at the corral gate. They bounded out of bed like a flash, shivering in spite of themselves, and peered out of the window, but could see nothing. They knew that Uncle Bob was up, for they could hear him. They hurried down stairs and found him carefully examining the trigger of an old rifle that had stood in the corner and that had not been used for years.

"Some one is out there on horseback, boys," he said calmly. "I think it's our man after the other pony. If it's High, I hate to shoot. You stay here, and I'll surprise the scamp a bit from the woodshed."

He slipped out, and the boys waited expectantly, both staring at the little window. There was the familiar squeak of the shed door, a whinny, and then Uncle Bob let fly his ancient weapon. They heard Mr. Standish in the yard and so cautiously ventured out. There, quivering and breathing hard, stood Harry's pony, but so far as they could tell there had been no rider. The pony had traveled hard and a long way, and was delighted to hear familiar voices again. He nosed Uncle Bob in a friendly fashion and whinnied his delight when he was turned into the barn.

The three sat a long time by the woodshed in the black shadow, watching and waiting, but were finally compelled to go to bed without further excitement.

They were all up at daylight again, and were

ready for the trail when the Supervisor and Tompkins rode up the valley with the pack mules trailing along behind them. There were two spirited chestnuts for the boys, and much to their delight the Supervisor seemed to be in excellent mood and most friendly. They traveled all day, with scarcely a halt, through timber that was magnificent. On every side could be seen the results of the splendid Forest Service. Three times that day they heavily blazed trees that were to be cut and burned on the return trip. Late in the afternoon they reached the bettle-scourged area. Everywhere there were groups of magnificent trees that were brown and lifeless. The Supervisor took the boys to a mother-tree and with the aid of his pocket ax he quickly cut away the bark and exposed dozens of little galleries in the wood, each one occupied by a fat white grub and his little pile of newly-cut wood dust. He then made some rapid calculations on his note book, then, turning, said, "Boys, if all that tree is as well populated as those four inches I have just exposed, that tree alone contains twenty-seven thousand worms.—Quite a hotel, don't you think? We'll certainly do some housecleaning in this beetle valley the next few days. Now, get busy, set up camp and get supper started, and we men will cut the necessary boughs for beds, and see to watering and pasturing the mules and horses.

We probably will be here a week, unless something new develops on this Florence robbery and murder."

The boys set to work with a will, using every bit of Scoutcraft they knew, and so well did things move that an hour before the appointed time everything was in readiness to put the supper on.

"Say, Harry, listen. I slipped a line and a few flies in my pocket, just for fun. That stream looks good to me. I'm going to slip off for an hour and see what I can do. They won't miss me, and if I can get the Supervisor a nice fish for supper, it will help. I've noticed he is much more congenial after he has eaten a good meal. You set up my little aluminum reflector and mix me just a bit of dressing—and, mind you, Scout, keep it out of sight." He slipped behind the curtain of low alders and was gone. Harry busied himself, and made every appearance of being very busy. Twice the men started back toward the fire, but noticed infected trees both times and stopped to investigate. The second investigation led them completely out of sight in the big trees.

Harvey rigged his line as he went, and when well away from camp he tried his luck. He was a bit impatient when he had no rises at all. He changed his fly and hurried on out of the little valley into the canyon where he was certain to find better pools. Just how fast he was traveling,.

or how far he had gone, he little realized. He
was just conscious of a great desire to catch three
fine trout. He entered the canyon with some little
difficulty, for the only opening through the cliff
was the one made by the stream by countless
ages of washing and grinding. Such pools he had
never seen before, and soon his efforts were re-
warded with a fine speckled beauty. He tried
again, got a splendid rise but, because of his im-
patience, lost him. He pushed on farther, to
where the valley widened out a bit and the pools
were more accessible. As he went he noted a
strange pile of new light colored rock up on the
side of the canyon wall, but so absorbed was he
in his fishing that he gave it not even a thought.
Besides, just then a splendid trout rose, took his
fly with a swish and was off into the deep water.
He had no reel, and only a willow pole, consequently it taxed his very best judgment to keep it
from snapping short. He played him back and
forth, working him into the breaking point and
then letting him have the line again.

He was standing nearly knee-deep in the cold
water when an alder limb flicked off his hat, and
before he could grab it it was out on the swift
current, around a great rock, and gone. He
chuckled to himself as he at last landed his fish.
It was a beauty—the finest he had ever seen. In
the excitement of the moment it looked at least

half again as large as it really was. He slipped
it into his bag, and was starting further down
stream when suddenly he heard a voice. It was
a wild, merry voice, that strongly reminded him
of an intoxicated man he had often heard going
past his house in Plainville. He stopped in his
tracks and listened. Yes, the man was singing
and talking to himself, and was coming straight
toward him. He slipped into the bushes and
waited almost breathlessly. He was able to dis-
cern a narrow trail now that led up the opposite
side of the canyon toward the pile of fresh rock.
He realized suddenly that the rock was a new mine
dump, or at least a prospect hole, and that the
approaching man was probably the miner. Perhaps he was drunk, and that was why he sang.
He had heard of such things. He was about to
step out and say "Hello!" when suddenly the
figure rounded the curve, and although the trail
ran obliquely from where he was hidden, he had
a fair view. A little gasp of surprise escaped
him, in spite of himself, and he crouched down
again as quickly as he had risen.

The man was tall, stoop-shouldered, and had
that peculiar droop to his head that he had noted
yesterday when the outlaw rode past him on the
trail. He could not see the face this time, but
certainly it was the same shabby coat and old bat-
tered Stetson hat. What a discovery! The

"wild life" had not gotten past him this time. But what was he to do about it? In a second the desperado would be out of sight and gone—perhaps forever. He must trail him if at all possible. He wound up his line, hurried to the trail and noted with keen satisfaction the prints of heavy hob-nailed boots in the soft leaf mold. This would make the trailing easy, so on he went, his every sense alert and keen, his nerve cool and steady.

At the top of the ridge the trail dropped down to a crude little cabin that was just below the prospect hole. He thought that he had found the hiding place of the most wanted criminal in the Front-range, and he was glad. Just ahead of him strode that tall, gaunt figure. There could be no doubting it now. It must be his man. Suddenly his singing stopped, and he gazed streamward a second, and then, with a muttered oath, slipped from the trail to the water. He leaned away out and pulled something from the water. Harvey watched his every move. In a second he straightened up and held in his hand the Scout's hat that had caught on a snag in the stream. He eyed it very carefully, turned it over and over, looked up stream a long time, listened very attentively for any strange sound, and then in silence went to his cabin.

"The price of carelessness!" groaned the Scout.

"I dare not stay, or the whole camp will be out . looking for me, and long before I can get them word, unless I am badly mistaken, my desperado will be far, far away, for he knows now there is some one in the valley, and probably realizes it's us, for he saw we boys with those hats on at the beaver dam." He was frightened a bit, in spite of himself, then after a moment's reflection he broke into a fast dog trot. He was a past master at the Scout pace and in a very few minutes was at the mouth of the canyon again.

"You wouldn't find that trail in a thousand years if you didn't know it was here," he said, half aloud, as he swung into the open valley and toward camp. He was certain he had been gone more than an hour, but because of the high horizon line he was unable to help himself out even by sun time.

The men were all seated about the fire when he arrived and were just preparing to begin the evening meal which, fortunately, the other Scout had gone ahead and prepared, even to the dressing for the fish. He noted the scowl on the Supervisor's face and promptly bethought himself of his two splendid fish. These he produced and exhibited with great pride.

"I am so sorry to have kept you waiting," he panted. "It wasn't the fish that kept me late, but a great discovery. But I won't tell you a thing until we eat. I've been running far nearly an hour and my stomach thinks my throat's cut. Here, Harry, dress this. I will clean this one, and they can bake while we eat.''

"Hurray for the Boy Scouts!" laughed Tompkins, good naturedly. "What did you discover, lad—the greatest gold mine in Colorado? Ha! ha!—a thousand other fellows have done that same trick in the last ten years.''

"Yes, a gold mine, and more, too," laughed back Harvey. "But let's eat. I tell you I am starving.''

The Supervisor ate heartily, and complimented the cook over and over again. When half of the big trout was dished up to him, steaming and brown, with a crisp slice of bacon laid on top and a spoonful of savory dressing at its side, all his good nature returned and he laughed and chatted like a schoolboy.

Harvey swallowed his last bite with a gulp, and then looked to see if all were ready to hear his momentous news.

"I've found the desperado!" He said it very calmly. "He is a miner, and has a cabin as cleverly hidden in the bushes as an oriole's nest.''

"The desperado!" cried all three men at once. "Here in this canyon?—Impossible!''

"Yes, sir, I saw him myself. I trailed him, I heard him sing and talk to himself.''

"Sing and talk to himself!" cried the Supervisor, in great excitement. "He was singing, was he,—tall and hump-shouldered—High Tucker, I'll be bound. And you saw him? Oh, I'm sorry. I was so in hopes the poor duffer would make his get-away. We did all we could to locate him, but I was glad we were not successful. There is a mistake somewhere in this deal, for I know High wouldn't kill a man. Yet, you say you saw the same man that you saw in the valley yesterday? Evidence is evidence, however, and our duty comes first. We'll go first thing in the morning. We can't leave our camp to-night."

"I understand it all now, Mr. Hastings," said Uncle Bob. "I got to thinking about it after that scare last night. It just must be High. He knew of my cabin, he knew there was a gun there, and shells. He rode the horse to the Upper Fork Trail until he was sure he wasn't being followed, then he got off and started that pony home again. He knew we could trail the pony to the fork, and then if he went on foot we wouldn't know which one of the four canyons he entered. The horse came straight home."

The Supervisor listened intently, then, turning, sharply, he said, "Boy, did High see you?" Harvey's heart sank, and also his head, for he must confess his carelessness again.

"Not exactly, sir, but he knows there is some

one in the valley. You see, my hat got knocked off while I was fishing and he found it in the stream. I was following him and I saw him pick it up. He laughed loudly and then went into his cabin.''

"Laughed, did he?'' commented Tompkins, shrewdly. "Well, I guess you saw High all right, but I'll wager my six-gun that if he knows you're here you won't see him again unless he takes a notion that you shall. He's worse than any pine squirrel I ever saw when it comes to getting out of sight in a hurry. But I don't understand it at all. He was always such a law-abiding fellow. It couldn't have been High, that's all.''

"Huh! If it hadn't a'been for a bit of carelessness we could go and settle it to-morrow,'' said the Supervisor. "If it was High, we must capture him.''

Soon the conversation swung back to beetles and beetle trees again, and the boys learned many interesting facts before their eyes grew heavy with sleep.

"Say, Harvey, do you really believe there are five hundred species of bugs that feed on the oaks alone and more than two hundred on pine and spruce?— Why, I never saw even one kind until to-day,'' said Harry.

Harvey made no reply.

"What's the matter?— Aren't mad, are you?" urged Harry.

"No, but you listen to me, Scout Carter. I'm going to catch that desperado and fool the Supervisor."

"Catch him how?"

"I don't know. I haven't the slightest, most remote shadow of an idea. But that doesn't make a bit of difference. Catch him I will, if that Supervisor will let me alone long enough."

The embers were burning low. The curtain of dark spruce hid everything save the tiny circle of flickering light.

"What's that?" said Uncle Bob, as he rose and yawned. "I thought I heard a fuss out among the horses."

"Nothing but that old mule biting Nellie," said the Supervisor, drowsily. "Let's crawl in."

They suited the action to the word and were soon busy unrobing—so busy, in fact, that they failed to see a tall, shambling, hump-shouldered man, with a sawed-off Winchester rifle in one hand, move back into the sheltering pines toward the picketed horses.

CHAPTER IV

"**B**UT we must capture him by night, if it takes a thousand men!" roared the Supervisor.

It was just daylight when Harry awoke from a very exciting dream only to find the Supervisor in one of his usual storms, and his apparent much-ruffled feeling so amused Harry that he hastily woke Harvey up to enjoy the fun, too.

"Sounds like that mule, Nellie, kicked him where his breakfast ought to be," laughed Harry. But Harvey, after one good look out between the flaps, resolved that much more was the matter with the Supervisor this time than one of Nellie's gentle pokes. Hastily he began to dress. Just then Uncle Bob entered the tent, a scowl on his usually kindly face. Instantly both boys noted that he was only partly dressed and what clothes were on bore every appearance of having been slung on in a desperate hurry.

"What's up, Uncle Bob?" asked Harvey, who had suddenly become eager and alert.

"Something has got to be done, and that sud-

70

denly," growled Uncle Bob. "We are getting careless, all of us. I didn't suppose a half-dozen real bad men from the State Penitentiary could cause the Forest Service so much trouble as this one desperado is succeeding in causing."

"What's wrong now, Uncle?" asked both boys in a breath, but he ignored them and went on hastily as he pulled on his high boots and tucked in trouser legs.

"I have never believed until now that our desperado was old High Tucker, but it must be so. That's all there is to it, after what you saw last night. Besides, no stranger would dare do a trick like that. Only a half-crazy man would come right into an armed camp like this one, manned by trained Rangers, and help himself to whatever he wanted."

"For the love of Pat, Uncle, tell us what has happened—what's stolen now—when, where, how? Every time I go to sleep something happens anyway." Both boys waited eagerly.

"We're cleaned out, lads," said Mr. Standish dejectedly, "cleaned out in the night. The Supervisor's pet mare is gone entirely—hide and hair. Every pack saddle in camp has disappeared. Every hobble has been cut to pieces and the horses and mules were all loose in the timber. The Supervisor has been rounding them up for an hour and he is wild with anger. Apparently the thief intended to stampede the loose horses, and, failing, took the best there was and rode away. Imagine any one stampeding Nellie! Mr. Hastings wouldn't have taken a cool hundred for that saddle any day. It was a present from the head of the Forestry Department in Washington.''

They were pretty well dressed by now, and emerged from the canvas walls just as Mr. Hastings rose from building the fire preparatory to getting breakfast started. On seeing the three watching him he was soon off on another wild tirade.

''They are all rascals, every mother's son of them—cattle-men and sheep-men alike! For ten years I've lived among them and seen them fight and butcher each other, but they have always been scrupulously careful how they dealt with representatives of Uncle Sam. I've never expressed an opinion one way or the other, and have warned my Rangers not to make such a fatal mistake. I've dealt with each one of them honestly and given them justice at every turn. I tell you what makes me hottest is that after all I have done for old High Tucker he would treat me this way, even when he is in a tight place. I've known for several years that High had been a sheep-man once and that in all probability he got that broken crown in one of their awful feuds. I've been thinking about it a lot this morning, and, come to think of it, the Postmaster at Florence *was* an old cowboy—worked for Templeton on the big round-up for years. At last, I'm satisfied High is guilty, and believe me, boys, I'm going to round him up to-day. I haven't ever meddled with their scraps, but they can't tamper with Uncle Sam. High knows it, too. He had his chance to get out, and he knows that now it's my turn."

"What you going to do about it, sir?" drawled Tompkins, who had ridden up just in time to hear the last of his talk.

"I'm going to High's cabin and arrest the crazy galoot in the name of the law," snapped Hastings, "and if he isn't at that shanty, I'll wait till he does come. Here we are, two days from headquarters and not a lick of harness to pull those beetle trees together with after they are cut; and how in blazes do you think I'm going to get back home with my horse and saddle gone? I'm going over to that shanty right after breakfast. Here, let's have a hand, Scouts—a few flapjacks and a swallow of coffee."

Tompkins shrugged his shoulders decisively and spat meditatively into the fire. "Still I don't believe it's High, sir," he said with conviction. "He may have a broken head all right, but there's too much sense in it for a game like this. No, sir, we're a-following the wrong trail. The blazes don't read right. I don't believe the sheep

and cattle war has anything to do with the matter.
I think it's Luke's boy, and his game was plunder
pure and simple.''

"No, sir,'' retorted the Supervisor. "We'll
have the whole thing out of High by noon, or my
name's Maud.

"Bob better start to-day on those mother trees,
cut them low and drag them pretty well together.
The young stuff is pretty thick through here and
let's guard it all we can. Better cut everything
that's infected and make it into piles. It's dead
enough to burn easily. You men do the heavy
cutting and let these Scouts saw the trunks into
about three lengths. Perhaps you can rig a harness for old Nell and save yourself a lot of slav-
ing, for she will pull anything you fasten her to.
Don't concern yourselves about me, for I'm going
to stay over in the canyon until I get High, if it
takes all winter. Better not fire your piles until
I get back.'' And he was gone.

"Well, I've got to have a couple more flapjacks,
boys, if I'm going to saw logs to-day,'' said Tompkins, and the Scouts returned to their cooking.

"I don't see,'' said Harry, after a moment's
meditation, "why these sheep- and cattle-men
hated each other so. Wasn't there room for them
both to feed their critters in these great valleys?
I haven't seen a sheep since we came and not more
than a hundred cattle all put together.''

"Of course you haven't seen 'em, my boy," said Uncle Bob, who had also helped himself to another cup of coffee and more flapjacks, "but if you had been here five years ago you would have seen plenty of them. You see all these valleys are a part of the U. S. Forest Reserve now, but in those days they were not. Now, every ranchman must have a written permit and pay rent for pasture on the range, and sheep are almost entirely eliminated, because we have found out they are too destructive to the range. However, there are a few flocks farther east."

"I can't for the life of me see," said Harry, "how a few sheep could hurt the mountains when cattle don't, or lions, or bears, or skunks. Won't you please explain?"

"Sure. Lions and skunks don't graze, lads, to begin with, and, what's more, they aren't at all fond of young trees or tender shoots as a diet. It's like this: the whole thing depends on the character and age of the woods in question. A young forest is never a place for grazing animals, and where there are steep slopes the damage from grazing is often very large. There are three great dangers in allowing extensive grazing, either for sheep or cattle, in an evergreen forest. Odd as it may seem to you, it is a very fertile cause of forest fires. It was a common practice ten years ago for sheep- and cattle-men to set fire to the forest, so as to open up new grazing lands, or to at least burn the grass over in the Fall to insure an improved quality of feed for the early Spring. Such fires did not usually consume the large timber, but merely killed it and burned out entirely the seedling and saplings. Vast areas of the best sheep-grazing land in the West to-day was once covered with a majestic growth of timber.

"Trampling is the second, and the third is browsing or feeding on the tender parts of young trees. Now you asked why the sheep-men so hated the cattle-men. It was simply because of the fact they both wanted pasture. It takes sunlight to make good grass, and in the dense wood there was not a very big supply of it; consequently good grassy meadows were scarce. Cattle graze without cropping the grass close enough to kill it, but sheep, feeding one behind the other as they do, crop the grass so close, and then trample the roots with their small, sharp hoofs, so that nine times out of ten it dies altogether. In order to insure feed for their cattle, the cattle-men were, as they thought, compelled to exterminate the sheep, and vice versa. You can readily see how this struggle for possession gradually became a bloody war, can't you?"

"Yes, but I don't see why one or the other of them did not go farther back into the hills and have the pasture all to themselves, without those awful fights.''

''Because, my boy, such action on the part of either party meant removing their stock so far from its final market that it ate up all the profits to get it back to a shipping point. Be sure to get the Supervisor to tell you of some of his experiences with the sheep and cattle war one of these evenings.''

Soon they were out in the valley busy at their task of cutting the beetle trees. Slowly the piles increased until the woods just surrounding the little camp took on the appearance of a saw mill. The air was filled with the sweet, resinous odor of fresh pine chips and sawdust. At eleven the Scouts went back to camp and began to prepare dinner.

''Better make a plenty,'' called Uncle Bob from the clearing. ''Hastings is liable to return by noon with High, and we will all have a life-sized appetite by that time.''

''He'll not get him, Bob,'' said Tompkins, as he stopped to spit on his great calloused hands. ''That is, if High is guilty. I, for one, don't believe he is. But, mark me, if he is, Hastings or no other man alive will find old High Tucker until High chooses that they shall. It's like going off to arrest a gray squirrel.''

''You may be right, Tompkins, but I think High

is the man. Who else knows this valley like this
man must but High Tucker? No one else has
ever lived in it but he."

"Oh, yes, they have, Bob. How about Old Luke
and his boys? The whole business looks a lot
more like some of their doings to me than any of
High's. You know as well as I that Luke's boy
hates every Forester with a fervor. What's
more, if he's in hiding in this valley he don't want
a band of men working in it."

"But Luke's boys have been in jail now some
days," replied Mr. Standish. "I brought them
back from my trip to their shanty. The Scouts
were with me."

"Yes, but didn't Mr. Hastings tell you what has
developed out of that mess? One of those young
men was not Old Luke's boy at all, but Johnny
Thorp. Do you mind, Widow Thorp's kid, the
sheep rancher from Rock Creek Basin? Seemed
he had been living with Luke and the boys, and
the cow puncher over at Murphy's picked him up
without knowing what they had. No, Bob, there
is one of Luke's kids, the older one—must be all
of twenty-seven anyway—at large yet, but all
three down in the jail refuse to tell where. They
swear they have not seen him for more than a
year. He was always by far the worst one and
would not stop at anything."

"Well, that may be true, Tompkins, but I'm

inclined to think Hastings will bring his man
back with him to-day. He does not often make a
mistake in his suppositions.''

"Dinner! dinner!" called Harry. "Two cars
to the rear. First, last, and only call!"

"How old do you suppose those beetle trees we
are cutting are, anyway?" asked Harvey at dinner.

"Well sir, boys," began Tompkins, "without
actually counting them, I judge they are between
one hundred fifty and one hundred ninety years
old."

"Without counting them—what do you mean?"

Tompkins laughed aloud. It had not occurred
to him that he was talking to green Rangers that
knew little or nothing of the growth or develop-
ment of trees.

"You see, boys, trees grow just under the bark.
That is, the cambium, or sap-bearing layer, is the
outermost layer, not counting the bark, and each
year a healthy growing tree adds a new layer or
ring. The inner side of the cambium layer forms
new wood and the outer side new bark. Thus the
older the tree the thicker the bark and the more
layers or rings there are. You have both noticed
these rings in old stumps or the ends of heavy
timbers, haven't you? Each one of those rings
represents a year's growth, so by acurately counting them you can tell to a year just how old your

tree is. You can count one after dinner and see for yourself.''

''Gracious!—a hundred and fifty years of growth, and here we are chopping and burning them like saplings.''

''I'll tell you at the fire to-night,'' said Uncle Bob, ''something of the awful struggle that is always going on in a growing forest for heat and light in order that enough food may be digested to make each tree grow. You have noticed how all the lower branches of every pine are dead, haven't you?''

Both boys nodded assent.

''It's because their needles could no longer get the necessary sunlight to change raw sap into food. It's one of the results of crowding. Two trees of the same kind, seeds from the same tree, in fact, and planted in the same soil, may be vastly different in size because of the conditions about it and the amount of light available. Millions of seedlings die annually in every forest in this struggle. Let's get into that other grove this afternoon and get it cleaned out before the Supervisor gets back with High.''

Early evening found all hands tired out with the arduous day's labor. All the afternoon they had watched for the return of Mr. Hastings. It was twilight now, and yet he had not returned. Supper was prepared, kept warm until dusk, and then eaten without the Supervisor. He had told them he would wait for his man and they need have no worry about him.

It had grown cloudy about four, and from the looks of the western sky some sort of a change of weather was about due. A cold breeze sprang up at dusk, that made the cheery open fire an especially inviting place; consequently as soon as supper was over and the few dishes hastily washed, the group seated themselves about it with the tent between them and the wind.

As the twilight settled in the valley the little camp looked odd enough, squatted as it was in the very midst of the fifteen piles of logs and toppings. After considerable discussion, the remaining horses and mules were each one tied to a great spruce not far from the back of the tent. Guns were carefully inspected and all was put in readiness in case the mysterious visitor should return in the night.

"Be sure and don't be foolish, boys," Mr. Standish said to them, "and shoot at Mr. Hastings. He's very liable to come blowing into camp in the night, and wouldn't particularly enjoy having you use him as a target."

"Tell us more about trees, Uncle," urged Harry, as he settled himself for the evening. "Harvey and I want to pass off our Honor Test for Forestry one of these days and everything we can learn now will help us just that much.''

''To-day you were talking about veterans and standards and poles,'' said Harvey. ''What's the difference anyway, or are they just names of your own?''

''By no means. Foresters must have regular names for regular kinds, classes, and conditions of trees, or else their reports, for instance, would mean nothing to any one save themselves. There is a very simple standard of names, and it is one of the very first things that you boys should make yourselves entirely familiar with if you are to be real Foresters.

''Any young trees that have not yet grown to be more than three feet high are seedlings. Trees from three to ten feet high are known as saplings, provided they aren't bigger in diameter than four inches, then small poles until they are eight inches in diameter, and large poles until they are twelve. All trees that are from one to two feet in diameter are known as standards, which means trees in the prime, or ready to lumber. Finally, any that may exceed two feet are called veterans. As a usual thing veterans have attained their best growth and unless timbered in a reasonable time will begin to grow dozy and rotten at the heart. You see, boys, there is no life in any part of the tree but the sap wood. The heart wood is to all intents and purposes dead, and being dead rots the quicker. Veterans are mostly heart wood and the growth is very small. It is important to remember, too, that in making this classification you measure your tree not at the butt, as you would naturally suppose, but breast high.''

As Mr. Standish had been talking the wind had been rising and it had grown quite chill, so much so that the comfort of lounging about the fire was gone, and at Tompkins' suggestion they decided to crawl into bed.

"We must carefully extinguish every vestige of our fire," said Uncle Bob, as he kicked the logs apart. "It's a bad night for fire. I think it will probably shower heavily before morning, but we must not take any chances."

Several buckets of water were poured on the embers, one last look at the horses taken, the guns placed in a handy position, and soon all was quiet in the tent. Even the green Foresters were fast asleep—dead to the world after their strenuous day.

The wind continued to rise until it was blowing in fierce little gusts and until every pine in the valley was sighing and creaking. Now and then the horses stirred restlessly and shivered. It was lightning in the south and the brilliant flashes every now and then terrorized Nellie, who pulled and tugged at her stout rope.

A little before eleven Tompkins awoke with a

start, hastily reached for his gun, and sat staring.
He heard Nellie pulling at her rope and stamping
the ground. He was so sleepy it took him a second to realize that it had been the lightning that
had wakened him. He tossed back the cover of
his tarpaulin and slipped out, gun in hand, to
make sure that all was well. Nellie promptly
brayed a friendly note and rubbed her big nose
against him, as much as to suggest to sleepy
Tompkins that he invite her into the tent for the
rest of the night. He saw nothing out of the
ordinary, but no doubt if he had not been so sleepy
at that moment, or if the wind had not been blowing so hard, he would have heard a faint whinny
in answer to Nellie's plaintive note. In forty
seconds, however, he was in bed again, sound
asleep.

It was past one. The wind had settled down to
a steady gale and every star was blotted out in
the inky blackness. Even the lightning had
ceased to give its occasional white glare. Harry
shivered. Some way his covers had gotten off
his feet and he was cold. He tried to adjust them
without getting up, but to no avail. Finally, completely out of sorts and in desperation, he rose to
a sitting position and arranged as best he could in
the jet darkness the covers, then lay down again.
He had just dozed off when Harvey gave the cover
a yank, almost completely uncovering him. With

an ejaculation he sat up. This time the tent was not nearly so dark. He wondered at it. As he sat it grew lighter and lighter, only it was a ruddy color. He rubbed his eyes as if to remove the illusion. Suddenly he forgot he was cold. He slipped to the heavy canvas flap and, lifting his lantern, peered out. The sight that met his eyes paralyzed him. He looked wildly about him as if for a way of escape. The piles of beetle trees were on fire! Everywhere he looked the hungry yellow tongues were leaping before the wind. He went to the back of the tent, and there the same fierce flames were rushing skyward. He was terror stricken. In three minutes their camp would be wiped out!

He rushed madly into the tent, crying as he went and pulling bedclothes from the sleeping men. Pandemonium reigned. It was for Tompkins to speak first.

"Grab your clothes and run for the stream. Here, take your gun and shoot—"

They could hear no more. He was gone, they after him as close as they could follow. Reaching the stream—shivering, clothes in one hand and gun in the other—they looked about blankly. Tompkins and Uncle Bob dropped their clothes and in an instant were returning. Harry heard Bob begging and coaxing the horses, and went to help him. In a few seconds the animals were safe, all save Nell, who stoutly refused to budge. Oh, how she brayed! They had never heard such an awful noise before. In a moment Tompkins returned with what was left of the smoking tent.

"I saved enough of it for a shelter, but it was a close call. I singed my hair badly. Bob, we must make one trip for a part of the food. Follow me, gather what you can and get back. I think it will be five minutes before the big pile just back of the grub tent gets fully afire. The grub tent is gone. It was taken down, or blew away; I don't know which."

Bob Standish followed, and so did the Scouts. Was there ever such a procession of oddly draped figures before! Quickly they gathered up all the grub they could manage and retreated. Tompkins rescued the axes and shovel and the cross-cut saw. When they returned again for another load it was too late. The fire was into the front of the pile now and the heat was too intense to get near.

"That fiendish scoundrel is watching the entire performance," said Bob dryly. "I'd enjoy shooting him full of holes just at this moment. Those piles were carefully fired by an expert—all lighted on the windward side and the front ones first. He deliberately planned to burn us alive, that's evident. We are lucky dogs that his scheme didn't work."

"What are you going to do about it?" asked

Harry through teeth chattering with excitement.

Uncle Bob looked wildly about him. "Boys, nothing under heaven but a terrific rain can save this entire valley. Oh, if it would only rain!" He almost sobbed it out.

"That's a pretty fine way to exterminate beetle trees," said Tompkins, sarcastically. "We are helpless. The wind is due east. That means straight down the valley—every beetle tree in the canyon." He laughed derisively, then turned away.

"If Hastings were here he would be wild."

"It will be very difficult to make him believe we could not have helped it. He will be cock sure we left careless fire."

"But if we had, it couldn't have lighted fifteen great piles of slash in a minute's time."

"Who did light it?"

"Old High," said Bob, doggedly.

"No," said Tompkins. "I tell you, no. It isn't like him. He never did it. It was our desperado, Luke's boy. He's done such tricks before, and he'll keep on till we leave or till we catch him. What we need is a posse of men."

They stood in silence, gazing at the sea of roaring flame. From somewhere down the valley Nell brayed.

"I feel rain," said Harvey.

"I smell it," said Tompkins.

Then it came. The ways of nature in the wild places are wild. Never before had they braved such a torrent of water from the sky as fell in the next few moments. It fairly dashed down, and clouds of smoke and steam rose from the valley in response.

They had gotten into what few clothes they had saved, and could do nothing more but wait as best they could for the coming dawn. It seemed to them it would never come, but when it did it was welcomed with a shout. Tompkins raked a few embers apart and with his ax cut dry limbs from across the stream, and soon things were hung about before the fire to dry and plans were being made for the coming day.

"It's no wonder Hastings didn't come home," said Mr. Standish. "His man was here. If he had only known he might have saved himself the trip. Well, every dog has his day, and High will have his. When we catch him, he should be shot without much delay."

At five o'clock there was a familiar "Hallo!" and all looking up saw the Supervisor crossing the ridge—but alone.

"What in thunder!" he gasped, as he leaned from his steaming horse. "I thought you had set the world on fire from the smoke that was rising. I told you not to fire till I returned."

"High's work," said Uncle Bob, tersely.

"Don't believe it," snapped Tompkins. "There's no evidence to that effect."

"High hasn't been to the cabin for at least two days. Only signs of life over there is the pelt of a good-sized grizzly hung out to dry," said Hastings, thoughtfully, and then continued with a growl:

"My friends, it's High Tucker, dead or alive, before we do another thing. You men have had a narrow escape from burning to death, that's evident. High evidently is determined to get us out of the valley by hook or crook. I had half a notion to force the mine and see what he's doing up there, but I didn't. We'll stay, however, until he does come back. I'll go back to the shanty to-day. He'll be sneaking in for provisions soon."

"We'll do some real camping if we stay long with what's left," remarked Tompkins dryly, "and anyway, sir, I don't believe it's High. I tell you what we need is a posse to scour this valley. I'd bet my head we would round up Luke's missing boy. The man that did this trick is desperate."

"But didn't the Scout see High here in the valley?" stormed the Supervisor. "What more evidence do you want? No one has seen Luke's boy for two years. Evidence!—what do you call evidence?"

"But I know High better than any of you," retorted Tompkins. "I tell you we are on the wrong trail."

"I'll bring him in this time, sure," said the Supervisor. "Let's get a camp set up and then I'm off."

CHAPTER V

"**B**UILD a camp out of that pile of stuff!" said Harry, disgustedly. "Why, Daniel Boone himself couldn't do it."

"I don't believe he could either," said Harvey. "It's us for home, for all that I can see."

"Home!" snorted Mr. Hastings in disgust. "Not a step until High Tucker goes with us, dead or alive. I have had enough of this raiding business, I tell you that, and we may just as well settle this thing now as some other time. Why, there is enough stuff there to build two camps and have some left. Tompkins, let's move over to the shelter of that second growth and rig a real Forester's shelter. I'm sure there is enough canvas in that old tent yet for that. Show these Scouts a few things about real camping. They have too much book nonsense in their heads. I told you this Scouting was all monkey business, anyway. These boys would starve to death in a grocery store unless in their guide book it told how to eat!"

"Seems to me that what we want first," drawled Uncle Bob, who had had a gloomy dispo-

91

sition ever since his rude awakening in the night, "is a bit of a fire—one we can manage and control," he added with a little chuckle. "Every living last stitch of duds any of us has, including blankets and tarps, are sopping wet. From the looks of things it's going to be a gray day, and we must have rest to-night. I feel just like I had celebrated my hundredth birthday."

Tompkins grinned sheepishly. "I've just been waiting for you to get to that very point, Bob," he said. "I'll bet my old wet socks that there isn't a dry match nearer than the sawmill, either."

"No dry matches!" cried Mr. Hastings. "Why not, please tell me? It didn't rain so hard that it wet right through the tin match can, did it?"

Harvey stood with his mouth wide open. He was caught again. When, oh, when, would he ever learn to be more careful? He had attempted to rescue the match can with an armful of other things from the commissary tent, but the can was hot and he had suddenly dropped it; the lid had, of course, come off and the matches had spilled on the ground and were burned. He had hastily picked up a big handful of them and had laid them on the lard can. Then the rain had come, and later, when he had found them they had rolled off in the wet needles. He was just about to tell what had happened when Tompkins spoke up.

"They all burned up with the grub tent, sir. I

had a few in my trousers pocket, but they are all ruined with rain.''

The Supervisor had been searching his pockets the while, and getting more angry as the truth of the thing came home to him—not a match in camp!

"It was my fault, sir," said Harry, straightforwardly. "I was careless, but I didn't know it was going to rain, and we were in such a hurry I hardly had time to think."

Tompkins' face clouded a bit at this confession, for he had thought to save the boy a scolding by his remarks; but inwardly he rejoiced in the manly courage that he knew it took to acknowledge his error.

"But," continued Harry, "if you will give me a chance, I believe I can make a fire, only it will take time."

The Supervisor looked at him incredulously. Was the boy crazy?— Make fire! Who ever thought of such a thing, and not a match in camp!

"Humph! Are you a patent cigar lighter, or are you just giving me some more of that Scout stuff?"

"No, sir, I can produce fire by friction, but it will take me a little time to find the proper material. Let the rest start on the new camp and I will begin at once to look for what I need."

"By friction, eh?—Say, what do you think this camp is—a chapter from 'Arabian Nights' or

'Alice in Wonderland'? Set up a camp! No, sir, what's the use until we are sure of a fire. Tompkins, bring me your mare, won't you, and I'll ride over to Duffield's for a fire. Building fires with friction!—if you were an Indian lad you might do it, but a civilized city chap and friction fire—''

Harvey spoke up. He could hold his peace no longer.

"But, sir, there are many ways to make fire without matches, even if you don't believe in friction. These hills must be full of obsidian and we have an ax. I never heard of a good woodsman that couldn't light a fire with a flint and steel. Daniel Boone could, and Kit Carson, and—''

"Robinson Crusoe and Jesse James!" cried the Supervisor, in disgust. "You want to turn the Forest Service into a Scout Patrol. Tompkins, bring me your horse, will you, and I'll be off. I can go and come in three hours. Go ahead on a new shelter as best you can.''

Tompkins ventured one more suggestion in hopes of saving the day for the Scouts' sake.

"What if Old High should put in his appearance while you are gone?" There was just a little scorn in his voice. "Think we better find our man first, and then talk of camps and fires.''

"But, sir, if you don't believe that we can build a fire by friction or with a flint and steel, I'm sure I can build one with your gun. Give us a chance anyway, for we have done nothing but talk so far.''

"I'm from Missouri, boys," said the Supervisor, in a softer tone. "But I like fair play, so go ahead with your obsidian and ax and friction, or however you do it, and let's get a flame. It's breakfast time."

In a flash the boys were off into the timber, each hunting suitable material. In ten minutes they were back, with several dead limbs of various sizes that had been chosen each for a special purpose.

"Now, Uncle Bob," spoke up Harry, "you take that piece of cedar, dress off all the outside that is at all damp, and then scrape me some very fine dust—see, like this: Just as fine as hairs. Mr. Tompkins, you take that large pine limb that was in the fire last night and dress me a bit of plank out of it a couple of inches wide and half as thick. Remove every particle that is damp."

Then, selecting a round, smooth rock with a bit of a cavity in it, he went to a large clump of mountain birch that had escaped actual burning but that had been dried some by the dense clouds of hot smoke, and selected a limb three feet long that had a natural bow in it. Then with the ream on the back of his Scout pocket-knife he deftly bored two holes, one at each of the extreme ends of the bow. Next he removed the stout whang leather lace from his own high boot and quickly tied the one end through the hole at the end of the birch bow, then running the other end through the second hole, he pulled it tight and fastened it. Next he took the bit of plank Tompkins had dressed out for him and cut a narrow notch well into one edge.

"Are you through with the drill yet, Uncle Bob? There, that's fine. Just let me finish it. Thank you! Harvey, you get a bit of dry bark from the under side of one of those old spruces, while I get things ready. Now, Tompkins, if you will get me an armful of dry twigs from those standing trees, we will soon be ready. We will move over to the shelter of that big rock," said Harry, confidently. "A little draft plays hob with a friction fire. If we had Mr. Tate here we'd get a flame in about a jiffy. He is sure a dandy at all sorts of woodcraft."

As he talked he had been putting a round, smooth end on one end of the cedar stick and a rather dome-shaped end on the other. These he polished reasonably smooth by rubbing them on the big rock. Next he shaped the slender arrow into an octagon so that the bow string would hold it the tighter and keep it from slipping.

"Now I have got to have a piece of dry cloth, and I'll be ready."

"Dry cloth!" laughed Uncle Bob and Tompkins together. "You stand big chances of finding dry cloth here, my lad."

"Why didn't you ask for a red hot coal, and be done with it?" laughed the Supervisor.

Harry's face fell. He was perplexed indeed. Was it another failure? But the other Scout came to his rescue.

"I've got a dry bandage and some cotton in my first aid kit. Hurrah, just the thing!" And he was after them.

The bandage was spread on the ground, the pitch plank placed on top with the notch just over the bit of cloth. The drill was forced into the bow string so that a rapid sawing motion of the bow would cause it to twirl very rapidly when held in place at the top by the smooth rock which Harry held firmly in his left hand. The other end of the drill rested in the notch. Harry was on his right knee so that his knee held one end of the plank in place, the other end he held with his right foot.

The cotton and small shavings were placed about the notch and the game began, every one of the little party bending over and gazing eagerly at the drill point and shivering every now and then in spite of themselves because of the cold, wet clothes.

Harry began the rapid motion with the bow. The drill burred in response. He then gradually pressed tighter on the stone socket and thus increased the friction.

One minute, a minute and a half, and then a shout of joy, for from the pan was slowly rising tiny tails of pitchy smoke. He worked all the harder, gazing earnestly at the pan for a spark, but none came. The exertion was tremendous, and finally the Scout was compelled to stop to rest and regain his wind.

"To much showerings," said Harvey, and they tried again but to no avail. They could not secure a spark. Harvey tried his hand, Tompkins tried his hand, and finally as a last resort Uncle Bob, after a careful readjustment of all the parts, tried his luck, but every effort was a failure.

They stood looking down at the fire drill, but no one spoke a word. The Supervisor opened his mouth as if to make some comment, but thought better of it and abruptly turning walked away.

Harvey asked for Uncle Bob's revolver. Mr. Standish was curious to see what the lad had in mind, so handed it over without a question. The Scout removed a cartridge and examined it carefully. Satisfied, he took his Scout knife, cut away the lead and stuffed into its place a scrap of dry bandage, then replaced the shell into the gun.

"Now you shoot it in the air for me and let me catch the rag. I believe the powder will set it afire and by careful blowing I can make a flame."

The idea pleased Uncle Bob and he did as he was ordered.

"I know what's the matter here," cried Harry. "It's that pitch plank. It gums up the drill and won't let the grindings out." In a second he was dressing a new plank from a bit of fir that was entirely void of pitch. He re-dressed the end of the arrow and arranged things again ready for another try.

Bang! went the gun. He turned to see the result, but to Harvey's consternation the bit of rag caught on a dead limb on its way down.

"It's smoking, it's smoking," cried Harvey, and he set to fixing a second shell.

Harry knelt over his drill and was just beginning to work it when a thought came to him. "It's a race now to see who will get fire first."

"Tompkins, give me one of those shells too." Quickly he pryed out the lead, picked out the wadding, and poured the little heap of powder among the shavings at the base of the drill. Zip! zip! went the drill. Smoke was rising freely now.

Bang! went the gun a second time, but Harry could not look to see the result. A minute lapsed, then he heard Harvey blowing. Suddenly he, too, dropped his drill, gathered up the bit of cotton bandage so as to make a crude bag, quickly covered it with the palms of his hands and began to blow also.

154800B

The men had caught the spirit of the game now, and even the Supervisor was interested. There was a little chuckle, and then a shout as both pieces of rag burst into flame. Both boys hastily knelt to the pile of twigs.

"I call that a draw," exclaimed the Supervisor, as the chips caught and the little yellow flames leaped into the air. "And I'll be shot at sunrise if you Scouts aren't the most resourceful boys in the world. Now, Tompkins, it's up to us to make good on that shelter, and we are going to do it before breakfast. We'll all have to turn Zoroasterians and worship this little fire and never let it go out, 'cause we just naturally might not be so lucky again."

Instantly the life surged back into the wet, bedraggled Foresters and in less than no time work was under way on the new shanty. A location was chosen just in front of a huge bowlder. Aspen poles were cut for uprights and set into the ground so as to form a box-like inclosure, the back poles just a foot and a half shorter than the front ones. A heavier timber was lashed to a near-by pine and then extended to the farther upright crosswise, where it too was lashed fast. Poles to support a roof were then lashed on top and the tent cut and fastened about the frame, leaving the front face toward the rock open.

Tompkins' tarpaulin was spread over the top to

form a roof. Some slabs of flat stone were set up for bunk legs and stout timbers placed on them to hold the smaller cross poles that were to serve as springs and a support for the mattress of green boughs. As soon as these were placed, the boys were dispatched to cut quantities of fresh boughs from a grove of neighboring silver spruce. Then just before dinner a shelf made from an old drift wood plank was added and the remains of the food moved into the new shelter. The fire was transferred and spread out so as to dry the bed-clothes, and all was in readiness again for a few more days of labor on the forest.

"Well, I sure take off my hat to you, Tompkins," said Harry, proudly, as he surveyed the cozy little shelter. "That's better than any tent I ever saw. The next thing now that desperado will be wanting is to move in. He could camp here all winter with a good deal of comfort."

"That desperado is going to camp in jail all winter, boys," said the Supervisor. "Let's get a bit of lunch, and while you rest and keep the fire I'm going to send Tompkins one way and I'm going the other, and we will pay High another visit. We have got to get him soon. If he isn't at the cabin we must form a miniature drag net and scour these hills for him. I won't go back without him."

After dinner the two set off afoot while the

Scouts and Uncle Bob settled down by the fire, for the chill was still in the air and the sky had every appearance of containing a first snow.

"What is this Honor Badge of Forestry I have heard you make reference to so often, lads?" asked Mr. Standish.

"Well, it's just this, Uncle Bob," said Harry. "To know twenty-five trees in leaf and be able to identify them in the woods; to be able to tell fifteen of them in winter when the leaves have fallen, then know twelve kinds of shrubs, and collect ten samples of different kinds of wood and tell what uses each kind are put to."

"Yes, we have to be able to estimate the amount of board feet of lumber in five trees picked at random, and must know about transplanting, grafting, spraying, and protecting trees from all sorts of ravages," said Harvey.

"Is that all of it now?"

"Oh, no," continued Harry. "We must thoroughly understand the three great causes of forest fires and how to fight each kind."

"Oh, you do, eh?" said Uncle Bob. "Well, that's all worth while information and we must get busy at once. But there is a great deal of other information that I want you to have also. There is a big lumber sale over in Salt Basin to be made very soon and I'll take you over there with me if I can. We will have to cruise all that valley before we mark it for cutting. The saw mill have bought a fresh tract and want to get ready to haul it after snow flies, and if we don't cruise it before we make the sale it leaves such an opportunity for the mill to cut thousands of unmarked logs."

"What do you mean by 'cruising' it, Uncle Bob?"

"Simply this: Two foresters go through and check the number and kinds of standards and veterans that there are, estimating as they go how many board feet each will make, or, to be more accurate, to estimate how many regular sixteen-foot logs each will make, and their diameter, then the whole is estimated into board feet.

"You see, only standards, veterans, spike tops and dead logs are sold to these mills, and careful check must be kept on them, unless the sale is big enough to warrant having one of the Government Foresters always on the job. The mill men hate the spike tops. They usually make only second-class lumber, and the dead trees are, nine chances to ten, dozy. Because they are compelled to take the good with the bad they often feel warranted in taking a few thousand logs extra to make up for the trouble. I know of one sale where the mill owner deliberately stole two million board feet of unmarked logs in one valley. Fortunately, our cruise books were complete and he had to pay or get off the forest.''

"I've been wet so long I've got to have some exercise or I'm going to be all stiff," announced Harvey. "I'm going to take a climb."

"Let's go up that mountain yonder," said Harry. "Perhaps we might stumble onto some trace of our desperado. Perhaps he is up there in that heavy belt of timber at this very moment, watching us build our camp.''

"Come on then, let's get started. We'll be back before supper, Uncle Bob."

An hour's climbing brought them out on the crest of the mountain and presented them a wonderful view of high cliffs and deep valleys, of great stretches of magnificent timber, and far to the north, at the end of an old road, rose Pike's Peak, her crest already snow-capped. They thought they had never before seen anything half so majestic or wonderful.

They sat a long time gazing down into the valley when suddenly Harry's eye caught sight of something moving. He watched it closely. The lights and shadows were so strong that it was a bit hard to see details clearly.

"It's a man!" cried Harvey, in excitement— "a humped-over, shambling sort of a man. And see, he is carrying a heavy pack.''

"Tall and—It's High, I'll bet my hat!"

"High, with his pack, going away," sighed Harry. "The Supervisor and Tompkins missed him. What shall we do? Shall we shoot?"

"That would be folly. It may not be High at all, and anyway, you could never shoot accurately at that distance."

"But suppose it is High!—He has slipped through our fingers enough times now. I think we should at least tell Uncle Bob. You know he said last night that no other man lived in this valley but High Tucker."

"Let's take a short cut straight down through that heavy aspen grove. It will save time."

They were running now, and soon found themselves in the dense aspen thicket; but on they went at good Scout pace, for they had a message that must be delivered at once.

"Stop!" called Harry, who had dropped a bit behind. "What are these?"

Harvey retraced his steps and there in the soft mud of the grove were fresh bear tracks.

"A mother and two cubs," said Harvey.

"By the great horned spoon!" ejaculated Harry. "Mr. Hastings saw a grizzly skin stretched at Old High's cabin, and it was fresh. Those tracks are at least four days' old. I can tell by the water that's in them. Two cubs! They must be young from the looks of the prints."

"Let's see where the trail leads us."

They were off again following the plain trail in and out through the park toward the stream.

"By jove," exclaimed Harry, "look at this!"

There, nearly six feet from the ground, on the bark of a shaggy old Engelmann, was a bunch of gray-brown hair—the unmistakable calling card of a Rocky Mountain grizzly. "She scratched right here," said Harry. "Old High shot her in this park. I wonder where those cubs are now."

They hurried on and soon came to the freshly stripped carcass where it had been originally skinned and covered with brush. The coyotes had about devoured all that had been left behind. Not a hundred feet farther on they suddenly came to a crude camp. Evidently it had not been occupied since the rain, but by the side of the ash heap lay a half dozen empty tin cans that were new. Hidden in the brush at one side were a half dozen cans of beans from the Forester's grub tent.

The boys looked at each other in amazement.

"Our desperado has left for good," said Harvey.

"That was him on the old tie road. He was carrying what provisions he could. He is gone."

"Let's hurry. Perhaps the Supervisor may be back and would want to know about this at once."

They were off again through the long aisles of tall white aspens toward camp. They were just emerging from the park when something scampered through the timber ahead of them.

"It's the cubs!" cried Harry, and he was off in quick pursuit. Although both boys followed hard they could get but an occasional glimpse of the two retreating bears.

"We couldn't take them if we did get near them," panted Harvey. "Let's return to camp. Desperadoes are more excitement, anyway."

"Yes, I know they are," panted the other Scout, "but I'd like to have a bear cub just the same. We'll bring Uncle Bob back with us at once."

In fifteen minutes more the new Foresters' shanty came into view, and as soon as the boys could get their wind they told of all they had seen and heard. Mr. Standish was greatly interested, but after a careful conference it was decided it was best not to act until Mr. Hastings and Tompkins should return. It would not, even in the light of the facts known, have been good policy to leave the camp alone.

"Let's take our rifles then and go back after those cubs. We have time," said Harvey.

It was agreed, and an hour later they were back to the old carcass again. Evidently the cubs realized in some vague way that there was a connection between them and the pile of half-exposed bones, for, sure enough, they had hardly entered the clearing when Harry sighted one, then the other, of the cubs nosing in the brush pile where the carcass lay.

They sneaked as close as they dared. The wind favored them, a great pine stump concealed them, and luck smiled upon them. They decided which would take which, then deliberately aimed and shot. Immediately they rushed forward to see what had been the result. One cub lay dead, but the other was gone. They listened and heard him tearing through the timber.

"I was dead sure of my shot," said Harry.

"So was I," said Harvey.

"Whose bear is it?" laughed Harry, excitedly.

"It's ours, of course," cried Harvey. "We killed a bear."

"And wounded another, I'm sure. Come on, let's follow."

They did, and after a half hour of chasing and dodging they cornered the half-starved, limping little beggar in a pocket of fallen timber, and after a desperate tussle, in which both Scouts got thoroughly "chewed" to say nothing of the dozens of long scratches, the little savage was subdued, tangled up in Harry's Scout shirt and tied with the aid of Harvey's belt and one boot string. Then started the triumphant march back to camp. Never before had two Scouts been so proud of their valor.

The Supervisor and Tompkins were both back, but were very glum. Mr. Standish told them carefully of what the Scouts had seen. They were puzzled, and Mr. Standish, at least, seemed angry. Beyond a doubt High had been back to the cabin during his absence, for the door was securely bolted and the windows latched from the inside.

The dead bear was skinned and the soft, young hide stretched to dry, while "Courageous" (for so they had already named the wounded cub, on account of his plucky fight for freedom) was fed and bandaged up. The bullet had gone through the fleshy part of the left fore leg, but fortunately no bones were broken, and with a few first aid measures "Courageous" was soon fast asleep on a blanket in the corner of the shelter.

Supper was eaten in silence except for an occasional question asked by the Supervisor concerning the road and the stranger. The dishes were done up by the boys, and the fire replenished, and then the boys were asked to again tell in detail just what they had seen. All listened closely. When they were through, Tompkins asked a question that set them all to thinking.

"If it was High's camp the boys found, why didn't he take that canned goods to his cabin, instead of leaving it in the brush? He wouldn't have to sleep in a temporary shelter, with no bedding, cold nights like these with his cabin not a

mile away. It don't sound probable to me at all.
I tell you, we must explain High's disappearance
some other way—may have been murdered by this
desperado, for all we know.''

The Supervisor thought hard a moment, then
he asked back:

"But how do you account for that bear's hide
stretched on the end of High's cabin and the carcass beyond a doubt at this other camp?—No, sir,
he camped there, so as not to get caught at home.
As for the bear skin, I can't answer. But I tell
you High Tucker is our man!''

"What's that?" asked Uncle Bob, rising and
listening intently.

"I didn't hear anything," said Mr. Hastings.

They all listened. Soon it came again, and it
was a strange sound for that part of the world—
the heart of a great forest.

"Sounds all in the world like an automobile,"
said Mr. Standish, "but there are no autos in
these hills, least I have never seen one.''

"It's a gas engine, that's sure," said Tompkins, "but just where I can't determine. You
know these pine trees act exactly like a wire for
carrying sound. The wind is right and it might
come from as far over as the Old Seven Lakes
road.''

"They do go in there in autos occasionally to
fish," added Hastings. "That must be it. Won-

derful how we can hear it away over here, isn't it?"

"It's on the old tie road, Mr. Hastings," ventured Harry.

"It is a pretty good road, I think," added Harvey. "Why couldn't an auto come in on it if it wanted to as well as on any other mountain road?"

"For what?" asked the Supervisor.

"For what, indeed?" they all asked.

"Why that roads ends at the head of the valley," continued the Supervisor.

"Just over the ridge from High's shanty," added Tompkins.

"Oh, it can't be on that road!" said the Supervisor, as if to close the matter.

"We'll go see," said Harry. "We can climb to the shoulder in twenty minutes and can see the road in spots clear to the end."

As they climbed, the burr of an engine toiling upward against a heavy grade was unmistakably borne to them on the breeze. Their minds were full of all sorts of strange questioning. The last twenty-four hours had brought them many adventures, and they were enjoying them as only live, red-blooded boys can. Just now their minds were full of speculation.

They reached the crest and sat down to watch, straining every nerve to hear. They had not long to wait, for soon they distinctly heard the changing of gears and whiz of the motor. Then they saw the lights, like silvery darts, flashing here and there as the road curved. There could be no mistaking it now—there was an auto on the old tie road coming up the valley evidently with great effort.

Should they hasten back at once?—No, better wait and see just what was its destination. What was the relation of the auto to the lone, humped-over traveler going in the opposite direction a few hours ago—that was what they were both wondering.

Nearer and nearer it came, harder and harder it toiled in its effort to make the rough grade.

"It's very dangerous to do that in the dark," breathed Harry.

"What if the brakes should fail?" asked Harvey.

"They knew all that, and came anyway for some definite purpose. I wonder what it could be. Why couldn't they have come in the daylight?"

"Look!"

Both boys were standing now, craning their necks. The lights were no longer lighting the road but were elevated at a sharp pitch into the sky.

"They are stuck!"

Just then the lights went out for a second. Finally they were lighted again, and the engine was started once more. Then the lights receded, as if backing down a hill to try again. There was the sharp squeak of brakes, and then slowly the car came forward again. This time the lights pointed skyward more than the time before, but only for an instant; then for a fleeting second they flashed in several impossible directions, finally lighting up the valley to its very depths, every limb and twig set out against the black.

"They are crossways on the road, or one front wheel is over the edge," cried Harry. "See! See!"— The engine stopped suddenly, there was the sound of sliding rock, a piercing cry, then the lights looked like two lanterns tumbling, tumbling. It was only a second, and then all was dark and quiet.

"They ran off the road, Harry," said Harvey.

"Some one got killed just then," said Harry, hardly above a whisper. "Let's go down to them."

"Useless, old man. Let's go for help, quick."

In thirty moments the entire Foresters' camp, with such relief equipment as they had, both Scouts with their first aid cases and the one remaining lantern, were pushing their way through the dark valley to the old tie road.

"What if we should find High?" said Mr. Standish, softly.

"But we won't," replied Tompkins. "He was never in an auto in his life, I'll wager that."

CHAPTER VI

THE auto was a complete wreck, as one would naturally suppose after rolling and crashing down nearly two hundred feet of cliff that was fairly bristling with sharp projecting rocks, dead down timber, and coarse tallus. The steering gear had been forced with tremendous pressure against the stranger's chest, and had, beside tearing his ribs from his breast bone, smothered his heart. He had died almost instantly, and was still pinned tightly in the front seat when the rescuers arrived.

"Surely this man did not come into these hills alone," said Mr. Hastings, as he gazed at the wreck and the dead man, made more ghastly by the yellow glare of the lantern.

"Let's look about a bit. The others, if there were any, were probably thrown out," said Uncle Bob. "Let's have that lantern a moment. We must all go cautiously, too, or one of us will go rolling over that next step-off. It's lucky the car hit that huge tree, for if it had rolled over once more nothing could have saved it from the stream, and then probably we would never have found our stranger at all."

"Here's a bag of something," called Tompkins, and they all hurried to him.

"It's the bag we saw High carrying early this afternoon," cried Harry, in great excitement.

"Then High is hereabouts," said Mr. Hastings. "Let's find him."

After a twenty minute search High's body, broken and bleeding, was discovered in a low cedar where it had caught in its downward course. The man was, of course, unconscious, but still breathing.

"That's the man!" cried Harry, excitedly. "I'd bet a thousand dollars."

"That's him all right," said Harvey. "And what's more, he can't get away from us this time until we let him go."

"Well, I should say not," said Tompkins, who was kneeling over the injured man and examining him. "He is very badly broken up. I'm not much of a surgeon, but any fool can tell that that left leg is broken and those scalp wounds may prove very serious. It is a marvel if there is not a fractured skull. These sharp granite rocks, you know, are not very considerate of even bone-headed individuals."

"Here, Scouts," called Mr. Standish,—"a make-shift litter, quick. Let's get the poor fellow up to the road and see what can be done for him. He'll die here in a few hours and we must find out a lot of things from High before that time comes. When it comes right down to it, I don't believe he is our man after all. Poor old codger!" Tompkins whistled at this remark, and both boys looked at each other in surprise.

In very few moments two slender spruce poles were cut and trimmed. The Scouts slid out of their jackets and ran the poles through the open sleeves, one in front of the other. A few extra thick boughs were stuffed into one coat for a pillow. Then the Scouts took their places—one at each end, ready for service.

"Better let us do the lifting, lads," said Mr. Standish, kindly. "It's some job to carry a man up a forty-five per cent. grade. I'm sure that even we men will have to relay him before we get to the top."

Reluctantly the Scouts obeyed, and soon Old High Tucker, yet unconscious, was lifted to the crude litter and started up hill. Harry made rough splints, while Harvey ransacked the wrecked auto for tire tape, for his adhesive had all been used up. In the search for tape, luckily, a collapsible canvas bucket and a pocket flash lamp were discovered, and soon the Scouts were picking their way to the stream in the inky darkness. They must have water at any cost, and that in the least possible time.

"What's the matter, Scout!" said Harry, from

behind, when Harvey stopped and waved him back disgustedly.

"No use, old boy,—foiled again! There is a cliff twenty-five feet high. The stream is at its base. We have no rope or ladder, and how are we to get down to that water?"

"Jump down," said Harry, jokingly.

"And jump back, with a bucket of water in each hand," retorted Harvey, disgustedly. "It seems like everything we undertake to do in an emergency fails."

"Fails—shucks!" said Harry, more seriously. "We came for water, and we aren't worthy of the name of Scouts if we go back without it. What shall we say to that Supervisor—'couldn't get a drop, sir,' and a stream within hearing distance? He'd simply roar."

"I've got it," cried Harvey. "Have you your pocket ax? I'll make a ladder of this tree."

"Sure, here it is. Now what?"

"See this tall spruce? Here, hold my legs till I reach out and catch hold of it." He lay flat on the cliff and extended his arm as far as he could, but he could just reach the tender ends and they broke off.

"Don't be foolish, boy, and fall over yourself. One dead man and one wounded is enough for once."

"Can't quite reach it!" groaned Harvey.

"That's what you get for being a little shorty."

"I have an idea," cried Harry. "Let's buckle our belts together and by fastening a stick in the loop end we can catch it out there in that crotch —see?"

"Capital idea!" shouted the other Scout, and in a second the casting line was ready. First time out it caught and soon the slender spruce was vibrating enough so that Harvey was able to catch a firm hold of the limbs near the top.

"Now, I'll swing out, Scout," cried Harvey, "and work my way down. You drop me the bucket when I call."

"But how are we to land you and that water on the cliff when you do get back up with it?" said Harry in desperation. "You will need both hands to hold on with."

"Oh, I know," cried Harvey. "I'll cut a stout pole with a hook on the end of it—a long trammel-like, and I can pull the top of the tree over to the cliff while you get off. See, you can grab this old root."

"Hurray!" said Harvey, and he began his descent carefully, yet swiftly.

Bang! came the bucket through the darkness and struck heavily on his head. He was off to the stream and then back again with the precious water, and then began the difficult process of climbing a very tall, slender spruce in the dark with two-thirds of a bucket of water in one hand. Harry thought Harvey would never come, and he could hear the men on the road two hundred feet above the cliff calling to them to hurry.

Although part of the water was spilled in the process, the trammel worked well, and soon they were back on the road again.

"Thought you both got lost," growled the Supervisor. "What did you do—distill that water?"

Neither boy replied. They were too near out of wind to answer such a question, and so just how that precious bucket of water was secured forever remained a secret.

Meanwhile Tompkins had opened High's clothing and had made him as comfortable as he knew how. Twice the injured man had uttered inarticulate words and moved a bit, but had not opened his eyes.

The Supervisor was lost in thought. "Got to get him out of this mighty soon," he said, at last. "Tompkins, will you go back for the horses? Bring the two best. Then you can stay here with High and I'll ride to Duffield's to get help, telegraph for a doctor, and report the accident to the County Coroner. Think we better leave that other poor duffer just where he is until the Coroner makes his investigation."

"Are you going to turn High over to the authorities?" asked Tompkins, dryly of the Supervisor, studying his face keenly as he spoke.

"No, I don't believe I will," replied Mr. Hastings. "I don't yet know what the connection is between High and this stranger, but at any rate the stranger is dead and can tell no tales. I believe High is guilty, but am not sure of it yet—that is, sure enough to turn him over to the law. I'd like to take him to—to your cabin, Bob, if your wife wouldn't object. She is a great nurse, and I want High near by where we can find out a few things. We could remove him to Duffield's, and thence nearly to your place in a wagon."

"That's satisfactory," said Bob, briefly. "I'm sure Belle would be glad to nurse him. She always liked the old fellow, and she told me when we started that she hoped we would see nothing of him."

Tompkins took the only lantern and started for camp. "Better send the Scouts along with me to guard that camp over there till morning, hadn't you?" he flung over his shoulder. "We haven't caught our desperado yet, sir, I'll wager it, and some one ought to be there."

"Yes, we have too caught our man," growled Hastings, almost compelled to stay by his former arguments. "But if you think best," he continued, "take them with you. They will be of no more use here. Scouts, what do you say? I'll send Bob back, too, just as soon as we get help here. You boys get some sleep and to-morrow we'll break camp for headquarters. Will you go!''

The boys were not very willing to leave the scene of action, but it was their Superior in the Service who was giving orders and their Scout training told them it was their place to obey without question, no matter how they felt about it.

As the three worked their way back through the valley and over the ridge to their old camp, Tompkins told them something about Old High that he had never mentioned to either the Supervisor or Mr. Standish.

"You see, Scouts, it's like this. You may think that I've been pretty obstinate about sticking up for High against the rest, even against so much strong circumstantial evidence, but I'm dead sure I'm right. Even if he is guilty I'd fight to the very last to save him. I'm going to tell you a secret, and you must keep it to yourselves. I like you boys, and I don't want you to think me just a crank, but the truth of the whole matter is simply this:

"I would have been shot by some one in these hills long ago if it was generally known who I really am. In fact, I have already been the target for a number of mysterious bullets that have always been charged to careless hunters, but you see it's this way. I, too, was a sheep man for years." His face convulsed at the very statement of fact, and although the boys could not see his face in the dark, they were conscious of a savage tenseness to his voice as he continued.

"High and I were on the same drive. I'll tell you all about it some day, perhaps. He was in charge of the herd—some ninety thousand head of 'woollies,' just think of it! And we were undertaking to force-march them through forbidden country, the valley of the Old Gunnison, to winter pasture. One day we found ourselves surrounded by one hundred masked, heavily-armed cow punchers, and were ordered by an advance guard to retreat at once. Old High refused, on the grounds that he was an American citizen and the range was free. He had a reputation for being absolutely fearless and a dead shot. We kept guard nights by relays, each bunch of sheep having its own guards. The tenth night out, when it came High's watch, he said he had heard horses pass on our right. I fell asleep again but in an hour I was wakened. High was not at his usual post. Something was wrong. I got the other boys up, and we left an armed guard at camp and the rest started for the fracas. It was a great stroke of fortune for us that I had wakened.

"The cowboys had captured High, and after a fierce, uneven fight, had tied him to a tree and were

just preparing to stampede our whole flock over
a rim-rock mesa that lay to our left by shoving the
near sheep over and starting the others in that
direction—a game that had been worked success-
fully many times and with tremendous loss. We
surprised the main body of cow punchers, and shot
up the bunch good and plenty before they could
rally forces. Then we found where they had tied
High after his terrific struggle for freedom. Of
course our first shots called all the cow puncher
sentries in to help, but they arrived too late, their
plans were upset. They had evidently expected
to have the stampede well under way before we
could get to them, knowing that after it was once
started any human effort would be useless and
they could then leave the sheep to their own destruction.

"There were at least four of those cow punchers
killed that night, and we lost one herder. We
knew, however, that it was just the first battle of
a long war to the death, for those dead cow
punchers had friends, and we were in a strange
country and could not abandon what flocks we had
at any cost.

"When we got to High, he was completely out
of his mind, for he had been struck on the head
with the butt of a heavy whip, and, strange as it
may seem to you, lads, he had temporarily forgotten everything he ever knew. His memory was

completely gone. Now and then a recollection of his earlier sheep war experiences would come to him and he would be rational for months, and then all would go blank again. Yet he swore vengeance on any and all cow punchers whenever a rational time would come, and they took pains to keep out of his way, for he was, as I said, fearless and a dead shot.

"I was a mere boy then, and in a way was a favorite of High's partner, the day boss. He did not want anything to happen to me on this drive, so he ordered me back to Delta with our dead comrade. Yet I knew it was as much to save me as the body of the dead sheep herder.

"The air was full of war—war all over the range. In one place in Wyoming seven herders were lynched to one tree and their flock of one thousand ewes and seven hundred lambs driven into a make-shift enclosure and clubbed to death in the night. Many worse outrages were perpetrated by both sides.

"Two days after reaching Delta I learned that Ike Jacobus, the brother of the postmaster at Florence, was one of the killed cow punchers in our fight, and that Hamilton Jacobus, his brother, was shot through the leg. You remember, Scouts, it was Hamilton Jacobus that was shot and robbed last week by the desperado we have been hunting.

"You see, lads, it looks dark for Old High,

doesn't it? For this story is known by many, and then the descriptions match. Dark, I say, but High is not guilty.

"Soon afterwards I went to Dakota, was there seven years, and then came back here and entered the Forest Service. Imagine my surprise at finding my friend and benefactor, Old High Tucker, working under the Supervisor to whom I was assigned. No one knew me. I told no one who I was, and fortunately for us both even High has never recognized me. Of course the Supervisor has never suspected, and he must not now; but I tell you again, boys, High is *not* guilty.

"There is one more thing I want to say. You have heard a good deal of Old Luke and his boys since you have been here?" Both boys assented eagerly. "Well, they were cow punchers in that same row and later took up sheep raising, grazing them illegally on isolated forests until driven off. They were active in the range wars for years and have a very bad reputation. They knew me as a boy, never as a man. But I'd best not tell all I know, I guess. At any rate, I have my own ideas about this Florence affair, and time will tell. If the right time ever comes I'll tell what I know. If not, I never will, for I am a Forester now, not a sheepman, and my life is too dear to me to throw it away in a useless feud. Yet, I will see High get fair play at any cost."

As they neared their camp they approached it cautiously, just for safety's sake, but found everything just as they had left it three hours before. They would, of course, never know that if they had stayed away but one more hour they would have found their new camp also in ashes. Their mysterious visitor had arrived too late to put his plans into operation, and besides he had not counted on their returning to camp before daylight.

After a few parting words of instruction and a personal investigation of the weapons left in camp, Tompkins started back to the scene of the accident with a bit of food and the two best horses in camp.

The boys were about exhausted, so after very few moments again disrobed and crawled into their bunk to await the dawn.

"What I can't see," said Harvey, as he turned over suddenly, "is, if it wasn't High, what in thunder was he doing in Uncle Bob's house or with our pony or with that gun."

"It's quite natural that Tompkins should stand up for an old friend, but I'm inclined to think we have our man," said Harry. "Looks to me like a new chapter in that old sheep and cattle feud." Then, thoughtfully, he added, "Do you suppose we boys might possibly be mistaken? You know the Supervisor is basing all his opinion on what

I said I saw. I never thought of it till just now. What if they should prove High guilty just on what I have said—and I might be mistaken! The man I saw up the canyon is the same one that is hurt. I'm positive of that, and he *looks* just like the one I saw on the pony that day, all but his hat—it's a different hat I'm sure. Do you suppose I might be mistaken and that there are two men after all?"

"Oh, I hope there are two," cried Harvey, "for we wanted to catch that desperado ourselves, didn't we?"

"We may have a chance to do so yet," said Harry, "if Old High is not our desperado. Say, wouldn't it be great if we could get High to tell us the story of his life as a sheepman. We will be awfully good to him at the cabin and perhaps we can get him to talking. It would help us to find out if we have made a mistake. I do so hope High won't die. If he should, we'd never know the truth, and if he *is* innocent the real desperado would be free."

"But how could he tell us his story if he has no memory, as Tompkins says? Why, he wouldn't even be able to remember where he was yesterday," replied Harvey.

"Yes, but he has rational periods, Tompkins says, and then he remembers all. He must be rational now, or how would he be in that auto?

Those men were coming in to see something about that mine, that's what I think."

"Yes, and the reason he tried to burn us up was so that we would not learn that he had a mine. They always try to keep the location of mines a secret. Desperado or no desperado, it was High that stole our grub, killed that bear, and set fire to our brush piles."

"But if it was High that stole the Supervisor's saddle horse, why didn't he ride it yesterday with that heavy bag he was carrying, instead of walking?"

"That's easy," cried Harvey. "He knew he was going to ride back in that auto."

"Oh, yes, but if High did steal that horse I should think he would have ridden it out with his load and then turned it loose, for he would of course realize that if he kept the horse by him at the mine sooner or later we would find him."

"Well, I wish," went on Harry, "that Tompkins had told us the rest of what he knows. Let's ask him to to-day if we get a chance, and tell him about our doubts. Perhaps he has some other suggestions. If what he has told us about High is all, then I don't believe he is our desperado."

The Scouts were just preparing breakfast for themselves when who should ride into camp but Toney Carson, the strapping athletic Ranger that the Supervisor had left in charge while he was gone. He had hardly unsaddled and watered his horse when Uncle Bob, worn and sleepy, came trudging over the ridge.

"Well, what brings you here, Toney—bad news from the cabin?" He spoke eagerly. "How in the world did you get here at this time of day— ride all night?"

"No, Bob," replied Toney. "I should have arrived last night, but late yesterday afternoon, down near Luke's tie-cutting camp, some one took a pot shot at me. Evidently I came on them unaware, for the shot went very wild. In a flash it dawned upon me that it was Old Luke's boy, who is probably the desperado we have been searching for, so I decided to just play him a little game of checkers and take him in. Say, that outfit are the slickest bunch of hiders I've ever heard of. I couldn't find the slightest sign of his whereabouts. I camped at the Deadwood cabin and went on a still hunt. Thought I could bait the rascal with my horse, but he wouldn't bite."

"You didn't see what he looked like, did you, Toney?" cried Harry, with a knowing wink at Harvey.

"No, boys, I didn't even get a glimpse, but I'm here and alive, and I have news. There is an awful row at the saw mill. Some of those jakes got wind that Luke and his boys were in the calaboose and that they had been fetched in by cow punchers. Instantly an old sore was opened and trouble began. They at once took sides on the matter, seeing as how some of them were old sheep men and others cow punchers. They promptly had two or three of the liveliest shooting scraps you ever heard of.

"One gang started off to take Old Luke out of jail and hang him, and the other gang started in to resist their going, declaring that they ought to let justice take its course. You know what happened. Well, the County Marshal thought it proper for him to slip over and take a hand, with the result he's in the hospital with a broken jaw, the jail has been raided and Luke and all the rest are gone. The thing is very serious, for there have been three fires on the lower trail in two days, and it's time you fellows are getting back to the scene of action. This little Sunday School picnic you have been having back here in the woods has lasted long enough!" and he laughed good-naturedly.

"It has that!" exploded Mr. Standish. And then he proceeded to tell Toney just what had happened to us on our little picnic.

"Harry saw High," continued Mr. Standish, "and we haven't had the slightest intimation that there was any other living man in the valley till now. This strange shot at you, though, bothers me. I told the Sheriff when we delivered Luke to him a few days ago that he better not leave him in jail long, or something would develop. He only laughed at me. Say, boys, you don't suppose Luke, his boys, and High could be in partnership on this raiding business, do you? It looks like it might be possible. At any rate we have High. He is too badly hurt to try to escape. We'll soon find out the truth. Fire on the trail, you say? Well, we'll get off home to-day. Hastings wants us to get there before he does so as to have things ready for High. We are to pack light and get out at once.''

So it came about that two days later, when High was moved to the Standish cabin, the Scouts were there along with their young bear "Courageous" to welcome him. Tompkins, upon his arrival, promptly called the Scouts to one side and gave them an interesting bit of news. "Courageous" wanted to know, too, but was only cuffed back by the excited Forester.

"A strange thing has happened, Scouts," he said, confidentially. "Old High's memory has come back to him and he has been giving damaging evidence against himself all day without being conscious of it. Every time I have suggested that he keep still and rest Hastings has gotten warm under the collar and urged me to let him talk, for fear he might not get well and then we would be no nearer a solution of this mess than we are now.''

"Then we'll hear High's story," whispered Harry to his brother. "You just see if we don't.''

High was made comfortable in the spare bed and Mrs. Standish took charge of him. The doctor had come once, and would be back before the week was out. There was no internal injury. The broken leg would, of course, heal very slowly. But the thing that was of all absorbing interest to all the men was the great change that had taken place in High, even to his facial expression.

Instead of being quite a diffident old hermit, such as they had known for years, he was now a friendly, talkative old man, wildly excited about his mine, yet filled with sorrow over the death of his friend in the auto. It was perfectly natural, then, that one evening a week later he should have said, with a confidential wink:

"Yes, sir, it's too bad, too bad, for Tip was a first-class fellow, and inasmuch as his dad and I were good friends, it seemed right enough for me to take him in first on that rich strike of mine. There is gold enough for both of us. His dad paid mighty dearly for my pig-headedness in that last sheep deal, and as I had to have a bit of capital to develop the mine, I just conceived the idea of taking him in with me. He drove over from

Pemberton in his car and I went out to meet him, and for fear he couldn't get clear in with that auto I took a bag of the ore with me so he could see it for himself. He was delighted, and of course wanted to see the mine right away. The car must have rolled over the cliff into the stream, didn't it?''

Bob and Mr. Hastings were watching each other out of the corners of their eyes. Tompkins realized this. He thought the time had come to draw High out in his own defense, so he deftly asked the question:

"Who did you say Tip was, High?"

"Oh, Tip?—why, of course, you never heard of him; how could you? Tipton Glaser, son of old J. M. Glaser, the former Sheep King of my early days. I was his foreman for years. It was really my fault that he lost so heavily, but I was determined to beat the cow punchers at their own game. It came near costing my life, too, though.'' He paused as if to recollect something from a distant past.

Harry nudged Harvey in the ribs with delight, while Uncle Bob and Mr. Standish pulled their chairs closer.

"It was an awful fight, boys. One of the very worst on the range. As I said before, it cost Mr. Glaser more than fifty thousand dollars and me a broken crown. So that was why I wanted to take the young man in and make him a bunch of easy money. He was just a boy in those sheep days, but he remembers. I've got gold, boys,—the real yellow stuff in paying quantities, up in that hole, but what good is it to me now? All the mines in this U. S. A. haven't enough gold to bring back Tip. He was an awfully determined fellow, just like his dad. He said to me he'd make that grade in that auto or smash, and he smashed. It was just like his dad when he says to me, says he, 'High, we'll take them woollies over the dead line into the cow country, or bust!' and, by gracious, we busted; but not till we had made coyote meat for some of them houndish cow punchers.''

Mr. Standish and Tompkins were listening with half-closed eyes, their chairs tilted well back, but the Supervisor was leaning far forward and there was an eager gleam in his eye. Very casually he interrupted:

"You say there were some cowboys killed at that time, High? Who were they, do you remember?"

"Well, there was Ike Jacobus, for one, and Ken Woodworth and Cap Dillon.''

"Is that so! And were there others hurt? I presume there just naturally was.''

"Yes, two, as I remember it now. Hamilton Jacobus was shot through the leg and some other puncher crippled in the shoulder.''

Mr. Hastings moved uneasily in his chair; then in a cool, steady voice he said, as he watched the injured man's every expression:

"High, did you know that Hamilton Jacobus had been Postmaster at Florence for the past seven years and that just a few days ago he was shot and killed, supposedly by—a—humped-over, stoop-shouldered, sheep-man, who is at this hour at large on this very range?"

Old High listened, his mouth wide open.

"By a sheep-man, you say?— My God, is that old feud still living! By a sheep-man—Old Luke—" He was apparently thinking out loud just then and not addressing any one.

"I told you so!" roared Tompkins, vehemently. "Old Luke's the man, or his boys."

High looked at him surprisedly.

"Oh, rats!" cried Hastings. "We have had Luke under our eye constantly for weeks and finally put him in jail. I realize that he is at large again now, but it could not have been he."

"But you did not know where his boys were," retorted Tompkins, with some feeling.

"All but one of them," snapped the Supervisor.

"And how many do you think it took to shoot up old peg-leg Jacobus, pray tell,—a regiment?" And then in his high feeling he forgot. "One sheep-man could shoot up a whole camp of cow punchers any day, anyway, couldn't they, High?"

Fortunately the true meaning of his remark was not appreciated by any save the Scouts at the time.

"And you were really in the great sheep and cattle war, High?" asked Harry innocently, so anxious was he to hear all the story.

High nodded in the affirmative.

"Do tell us all about it," urged Harvey.

"In light of present facts it would be interesting," urged Hastings, and as all were eager High consented.

"It started long ago, boys,—as far back as the seventies. An occasional sheep-man would appropriate a stray beef or adopt a few mavericks, then a band of whisky-happy cow punchers would riddle a trespassing herder. But such minor incidents never really marred the general serenity.

"It wasn't until the settlers began coming in large numbers that real trouble set in. They, of course, chose the best land for homesteads and put up fences to protect their stock and little homes. The fencing of grazing lands made it impossible for great herds to run, so the cattle kings did everything in their power to suppress the settler. Range and feeding ground grew scarce. Then some folks, knowing that sheep could subsist and get fat on land that would let cattle starve, began bringing in sheep. They flourished and grew in numbers tremendously and paid enormous dividends.

"Now it soon developed that cattle would have nothing whatever to do with pasture that had been largely grazed over by sheep, so the feeling grew between the two parties until finally the great sheep and cattle raisers got together and divided range, making a dead line, over which neither one was to trespass. Then there came dry seasons, and the only available pasture lay farther back in the forest, nearer to the retreating snows. Thither the sheepmen endeavored to take their sheep. The war was on. A few capitalists had divided the whole western range for their own convenience, and expected smaller raisers to abide by their decisions without so much as consulting them.

"One sheep raiser crossed over the dead line and took his sheep into the Big Piney valley, famous for its cattle raising. He was attacked by cow punchers at night, the herders were tied to trees without any ceremony, and the flocks clubbed to death while the grub outfits were burned. But the sheepmen were determined. Others attempted the same game, and flock after flock were stampeded over the edge of the rim-rock mesas of which the sheep country is full. The two factions began naturally to organize. The range belonged to the Government and both parties were entitled to use it. Wool was just as necessary as beefsteak, and so the feud grew in scope and strength.

"Then came the uncalled-for murder of 'Pete Swanson,' who had taken one thousand sheep into the high hills for pasture in order to save them from starvation. He was warned to get out, but he flatly refused. Then masked men rode in upon him and ordered 'Hands up!' But instead, up went Swanson's rifle. 'I'm an American citizen! I'll stand by my rights!' he cried. He was shot dead, and his entire herd clubbed to death; and although ten thousand dollars was offered for the backguard, he was never taken."

"Were you mixed up in any of those awful feuds, High?" asked Harry.

"That I was, lad. I was a foreman for Glaser, one of the largest of the sheep herders. Once I started with twenty thousand head of sheep to cross Delta County into Mesa County. I went up on a bluff to do guard duty while my herders rested and slept, for we had been on watch night and day and were worn out. Just as I reached the top I saw twenty masked cow punchers ride in and begin to tie my herders. I knelt and raised my rifle, determined to clean them out. I could have gotten six—maybe half of them, but they would get me later, and at home was the wife and kids. They stampeded my flocks and I saved less than a thousand head. Later, while I was away, these same punchers, both Jacobus boys among them (I could see them plainly from my higher point with my glasses), rode to my own cabin in my absence and set fire to my house and barn, tore down my corrals, and frightened my wife until she died in hysterics.

"I became a nomad whose main business it was to fight cowboys. Many's the time I've shot at them from ambush."

"Careful, High," said Tompkins, a black scowl on his face.

"And sometimes not from ambush, High?" pressed Hastings, his eyes tiny beads of burning light.

"Yes, both," replied High, calmly, then adding, "But that was long, long ago, boys. The sheep and cattle war is over now and I've been a peaceful man these last years."

"Yes, and then you did what?" pressed Uncle Bob. "Tell us how you came to get that wretched blow on the head that affected all the rest of your life."

"I took another flock, and Tob Barnes went with me. We started for Utah. I got notice to get out from the cow men. I went back, got more rifles and two thousand rounds of ammunition. We got other sheep men interested and we planned a great united drive, all going together—more than one hundred thousand head of sheep.

"Tob and I were in charge—one by day the other by night, and as the guards were posted each night, and the black sheep put out to the edges of the great woolly mass as markers, we would call, 'Remember Swanson!' It was our pass word.

"We were well started when we heard that a hundred cow punchers had pledged themselves to annihilate sheep and herders alike. We divided into bunches, each with his own grub wagon, and moved, one just ahead of the other. By careful maneuvering we got as far as Whitewater. Old Luke and his boys were in charge of one of the great flocks from Gunnison, and they were not afraid of all the cow punchers in the West, for they had been cow-men in former years and knew their brand. At Whitewater some of our herders got crazy drunk on whisky which the cattlemen generously gave them, consequently our guards were a bit disorganized. Directly to our left lay a great rim-rock, and unfortunately we were compelled to stop there to rest and sober up. It was the cowmen's coveted chance and they made the most of it.

"The punchers came in the night. They had evidently planned an enormous stampede, but there was a young chap among our herders that slept with his ears to the wind. He heard strange sounds, so getting up and finding me gone from my usual post he gave the alarm. The herders came to my rescue, but I was hard set. I fought six of them and was all right as long as I could keep them in front of me. They dared not shoot for fear of bringing the herders from the other bunches that were camped along the rim-rock. They finally overpowered me by striking me on the head with a very heavy quirt butt. It was that blow that affected my mind. We saved a part of our sheep and force-marched them to Utah, but I was no good, for I could never remember accurately, and at times not at all.

"Old Luke tried to see a flock through again the next year, but they got his sheep, every one, and nearly finished him. He swore then and there eternal vengeance on every cow puncher that should ever cross his path, and I've heard it said that he has at least a half dozen cowmen to his credit, all of whom were in that attacking party. But that may just be boast.

"After the rustlers war I lost all I had, and my only friend, Mr. Glaser, was shot from ambush. So I struck for the mountains, and I've been here ever since, just puttering around, prospecting and washing on the range. I love the open and the big solitudes. I can't bear a civilized bed. I haven't slept in one for years till now.

I know I'd get better sooner if you would just put me out yonder under that big silver spruce. There is strength in the ground, boys, lots of it.

"It seems so strange to be telling you this story. It's the first time I have been able to remember it all at once since that awful night. Some way a hundred little incidents have occurred to me that I have not remembered for years and years just in these last few days since the excitement that came to me over my great gold strike."

"High," said Mr. Hastings, "I was over to see you the other day, but you weren't home. Where do you keep yourself all day and night?"

"You were?—Why, that's strange. I must have been to the mine. I've been working very steadily there now for some months, night and day much of the time, following up my new vein."

"Where did you get that big grizzly skin that hangs on the cabin?" continued Hastings, carelessly. "Must have shot it recently."

"I didn't shoot it at all," said High. Tompkins noted that there was no concern on High's face as he said it.

"How did you get it then, pray tell—sprinkle salt on its tail?" said the Supervisor, scornfully.

"You may think it strange, boys, but to be perfectly honest with you I'm not just sure where that bear skin came from. I remember it's there. I remember about a man being at the cabin—said he knew me well, and all that, but I couldn't remember him, and I was afraid he was just nosing about to see what I was doing at the mine. I remember of finding a haunch of bear meat at my cabin door and the hide stretched to dry, but to save my life I don't know how it came there."

"Those were great beetle trees we cut over in the valley. Too bad to have to get rid of them," said Uncle Bob, trying to lead High out on a different line and confuse his story.

"Cutting beetle trees, were you? I was wondering what brought so many of you up into that valley just at the time of the accident, but I forgot to ask. Yes, it beats all how the pest will break out if you don't watch it. I used to take great pride in being able to locate them trees, but I haven't paid much attention to them lately."

"I saw a boy's hat—brown felt, hanging in your cabin, High. Is that your boy's?" asked the Supervisor, shrewdly.

"Oh, no, Hastings, my lad is dead. I picked that hat up somewhere,—out of the stream I think. Some hiking party lost it, I suppose."

Tompkins laughed outright.

"What you laughing at, Tompkins?" said High, crossly. "Do you think I'm lying?" His face was flushed now, and he noted for the first time the intense expression on all faces.

"What made you ask me so many little questions, Hastings? What's up? You don't suspect I'm crooked, do you?"

"High, you puzzle me greatly. You are so different to-day than you were a month ago. You seem like a different man. I was always your friend, though, was I not? It was I that had you removed here. Why question my friendship for you? I have been a better friend of yours than perhaps you will ever know."

"What do you mean, sir?"

"Say, High, answer me just one more question. Have you had in your possession lately, or have you seen anything of, a sawed-off Winchester?"

"Why, Bob; it is in my cabin now," said High, slowly.

Every one sighed audibly, and the Supervisor jumped to his feet and faced Tompkins, whose face wore a strange look of mingled surprise and disappointment.

"But it is not my own, of course," added High, slowly. "You remember my gun, Bob,—you have seen it very often."

Mr. Standish nodded.

"Well, I used mine very little, but always kept it in good condition and handy. Last week I went to get it and it was gone. In its place stood Bob's old sawed-off Winchester. That was what

first told me you were somewhere in the valley.
I supposed something had happened to your own
and that you had just borrowed mine. I was
so busy at the mine that I gave the matter
very little thought. You left it there, didn't you,
Bob?"

"No," said Mr. Standish, "I did not. It was
taken from my cabin a few days ago by a hump-
shouldered, tired-eyed desperado,—the man, no
doubt, who shot and killed Jacobus at Florence.
He must have taken it to your cabin."

The color faded from High's cheeks. Suddenly
he understood the meaning of the questions. A
deep anger flushed his face and he eyed the Supervisor, but all he said was:

"Remember, Hastings, Jacobus was a cattleman with a record, and no doubt deserved all he
got. Sheep-men are loyal to each other."

"Yes, but that doesn't satisfy the law," retorted Mr. Hastings. "What we want is the man
that did the shooting—and we think we have our
man located."

"You will never find your man, sir," said High,
as if to close the matter. "Sheep-men don't get
caught."

"We'll see," said Hastings.

We rose to go, all but Tompkins, and he hung
back to say a word to High.

"High isn't our desperado," whispered Harry,

"and I'm so glad.   Oh, isn't he great!   We must help him all we can."

"The only way we can save him is to catch the real desperado," said Harvey.   "Oh, I wish we could, but I don't know where to begin."

CHAPTER VII

"I DON'T know what to think, Bob," Hastings was saying as he stood at the gate preparatory to leaving. "I am morally certain that High is guilty, but how we are ever going to prove it is more than I know. I'll tell you confidentially what I think happened. High went to Florence and took samples from his hole in the ground to have them assayed. He probably just stumbled onto Jacobus while there and, recognizing him, up and blazed away. It was the way of the range in those other days. He made his get-away then and forgot he ever did it. He doesn't remember it yet. He may never remember it again, and if he doesn't—well—"

"Of course that may all be true," said Uncle Bob, slowly, and with much hesitation, "but frankly, sir, I don't see how, in the light of what we know, it could be true. However, sir, we shall see that no one interviews him, as you request, and will await developments. I wish that some of us could have stayed up there in the valley a few days longer to see what would happen after we once got our hands on High. You know, I have been wondering over and over who it was that shot at Toney as he came to us, for Luke surely would not stay in the valley after his escape.''

"Oh, that was just a happenstance, Bob, nothing more. Some one shooting squirrel or something else. You see if there had been any criminal intent they would certainly have tried again, or at least made more certain with the first shot.''

"Yes, but if he came onto them suddenly perhaps they might have fired hastily.''

"I don't take a bit of stock in this talk about Old Luke's other boy being in the neighborhood. No doubt he *is* somewhere, but he knows too well that there are a hundred hands against him here, and he will keep himself scarce of these parts I'll warrant you.''

"Perhaps so, perhaps so,'' added Bob, dubiously, "but you must not lose sight of this fact: It was the Forest Service that turned Old Luke over to the law, and so far, outside of this episode at Florence, all the damage that has been done has been directed against your camp and mine—in other words, against the Forest Service. Now, if High was on a rampage it seems more than likely to me that he would have given some of the mountain ranchmen over in Beaver Canyon a little trouble, too, along with ours, as he had no grudge against the Service, or you or I, and if he has struck gold he would not need to steal. Mr.

Hastings, there is a skunk in our woodpile somewhere. Things just naturally don't smell right to me. We are woefully short of facts and are working in the dark."

"Well, we'll see if that ghost will appear any more now that High is taken care of," said the Supervisor, as if to close the matter. "Now for business: Bald Knob Valley has to be cruised at once. My! but I hate to see that splendid growth of Western yellow pine and lodge pole cut. We have cared for it night and day these long years and it has been the pride of our division. But, of course, I realize also that it's full of prime 'standards' and 'veterans,' and it's as much a part of good forestry to sell them when they're ripe as it is to bring them to the ripe condition.

"That Harbaugh concern that cut that big tract on Turkey Creek last spring has made application for five million feet, and that means work for us all. It also means that the big mill will be moved in and that they will go after it hard when they do start. It doesn't take long now-a-days to strip a valley of its best trees with those confounded little donkey engines, steel skid-cables and a train of cars. Two saw mills in the valley will keep us busy.

"They want to put the mill in on the stream just where the growth of aspens stood and run their main track straight back through the valley.

They will cut both sides of the slope at once and yank their logs down to the track with the donkey engine and cables. It beats the old-fashioned horse skidders all to pieces. It's awfully hard on the small stuff and seedlings, but what are you going to do? They are planning on cutting ties out of the tops, and they want to leave the burning of their slash piles until snow falls. That means we must watch it night and day, and also that somebody has got to go right over to that camp, live there and keep check on ties and saw logs. I trust Old Harbaugh all right, but those cutters, you can't tell a thing about them."

"Yes, sir. Who is to go?" asked Mr. Standish. "It looks like it's up to Toney or Tompkins. I can't go, for I must be getting after those seed for the nursery at Palmer Lake. Then, too, there is that little sale over in Grass Valley that we have been standing off, and that matter about grazing in Upper Box Canyon. You can't go, of course, and I declare it seems too bad to take Toney off the two trails, for with this gang of mill hands hunting the woods on Sundays and coming and going with their pipes, I'm afraid we will be kept busy. Then, too, don't forget Luke is out and he will get even. Let's offer a reward for his arrest at once."

The Scouts had been helping Tompkins harness, and now came toward the two Foresters, leading the horses.

"Can't have Tompkins," Hastings was saying. "He must get at the reports at once and look after those experiments we have been conducting for the State Forester relative to the Ichneumon Fly. I don't suppose you would be willing to have the Scouts go over there a few weeks, would you, Bob? One boy could check logs and the other keep his eyes open about the slash and keep us posted as to the condition of the young stuff. They would be certain of excellent treatment, because they would be there as representatives of Uncle Sam. It would be a great experience for them, Bob, just like going to school. They would learn a thousand little things that would make them good foresters later. You know it strikes me they are the stuff future foresters are made of anyway."

"Well, Scouts," cried the Supervisor merrily, "now you are back for real work again on the range. You will have to let Old High tame that cub for you and you get into the real harness. Your uncle here has a proposal to make to you, and I just want to say, you have made good with me. I believe in you both. I have tried very hard to make you boys cross. I was just testing you to see what you were made of. I tell you, you have the real Scout spirit, and if you are as eager to learn this next month as you have been these past two weeks then you are going to have a great opportunity now.''

Uncle Bob opened the plan to the boys, and Tompkins, seeing all were occupied, hastily excused himself and went to the cabin again, supposedly to get his gloves. Aunt Belle was just coming down the path, and as he passed her he thanked his lucky stars for his good fortune, for he had been wondering all the morning how he was to get a few words with High alone before he left. He hurried in, and there was a gleam about his eye that was almost fierce.

"High,"—the old man turned sharply, a look of inquiry on his face, "I've just got about two minutes—listen! I want you to get every word I say and keep it to yourself. For your own sake, believe it's the truth that I'm telling you.

"You are at present in a net of circumstantial evidence that it is well nigh impossible to get you out of. The law is looking for you. Hastings believes you shot and killed Jacobus at Florence, and has some strong evidence to that fact—you were in Florence, and you know it, so does he; Jacobus was a cattleman, you are a sheepman; you perfectly well know that that last feud became notorious; everybody that knows anything about the range wars at all knows that you took solemn oath to kill every cow man that ever crossed your path—'' He was tearing on at a terrific rate, his clenched fist bobbing up and down under poor Old High's protesting face.

"Now, I know you are innocent, but I can't prove it yet. I am the Tompkins—the young chap you ordered back to Whitewater with Parkinson's dead body. I am your friend. I will not fail you. But listen, man, you babble like a school boy. You talk like a graphophone. You tell all you know, and then some. Now, my good friend, listen to me. You are lost, absolutely lost, and all the king's horses and all the king's men can't save you unless you shut up. Keep still. Do you hear me? You don't know anything more about anything or anybody. If you fail on your end of the bargain, remember, you'll hang, High. The people of these valleys are sick and tired of this killing business and you wouldn't have a ghost of a show with any jury that might be gotten together in these hills. I'll do my best. These Scouts know all about it. They are your friends. You can trust them. But don't talk.''

High watched him disappear through the door and then settled himself down to think. The more he thought, the greater the confusion that crept into his mind, until he just sat and stared. He could not comprehend it all. A week ago he struck gold, and to-day he was being hunted by the law for a murder he had never heard of before.

The boys were delighted at the prospect of their new work. For nearly a week they worked with Toney and Uncle Bob, completing the new Forestry trail that was to join the West Beaver Reserve with the East Beaver Reserve. Sometimes it was drilling a path on solid rock, sometimes up long zig zag slopes of sliding tallus, or again down through little green valleys of quaking aspens or through the long avenues of pine and spruce. It was vigorous work, but they were learning much and it was getting them thoroughly seasoned in arm and limb for the long days when the mill should come.

At night they took much pleasure in feeding and romping with the cub, who had been chained with a stout chain and collar to a pine just away from the porch. At first the bear was very shy and would become very watchful when the lads came near. Invariably he would whiff the air and when they drew close enough smell and smell of everything they had on. At such time he would act so queerly that the boys could not make it out. They noted, however, that he went through the same performance no matter who came near him.

Once Mr. Harbaugh had occasion to come to the cottage on business, and happened to come when

the cub was asleep. Suddenly he awoke with a
yelp and bounded in a single leap to the end of
his chain. So violently did he jump that the chain
suddenly tightened out and threw the cub to the
earth with terrific force. He gathered himself
together, his hair on end, his whole body quivering
with fear, his eyes tiny balls of fire and every
muscle alert.

High spoke to him kindly, and at the sound of
a familiar voice he sneaked over to the chair and
lay down, half ashamed of himself, yet whining all
the while.

"That cub has a powerful dislike for some odor
or other," observed High, "and he thought for
just a second you had some of it on you. I don't
know just what it is, but that cub has a powerful
good smeller and he doesn't propose to get too
near to anything that don't smell just right."

"Courageous" was keen of wit and soon
learned to play like a fat and well-fed puppy. He
ate everything placed before him and begged for
more, so grew amazingly fast, and before the boys
could realize it their cub was changing into a powerful grizzly bear that was perfectly friendly to
all whom he knew, but very fierce and terrifying
to every stranger until he had entirely satisfied
his smeller that the new party was in no way
identified with some terrible odor that haunted his

sensitive nostrils. He was an extremely curious
bear, and it was almost painful to watch him when
new folks or objects came for the first time into
his world—his curiosity urging him on to investigate and his horror of some dread smell hold-
ing him back as if by a mighty chain.

One fine morning the Scouts awoke to find the
valley fairly wiggling with yellow and brown
caterpillars. Aunt Belle promptly forbade any
one from drinking the water until it had been
boiled, and Uncle Bob spent two hours investigating and making a report.

"Gee, the birds will have a feast to-day!" said
Harry to his uncle.

"They sure will. It's Thanksgiving in Bird-
ville to-day," added Harvey.

"That's just where you are all mistaken,"
laughed Uncle Bob. "A bird never eats a yellow
caterpillar. Yellow is a sign to all birds that the
worm is sour and bitter, and he leaves it absolutely alone. That's why birds don't eat bees and
wasps—same yellow sign. No, lads, they must
be gotten rid of in some other way. Nature keeps
all of her wild life balanced to a nicety, except
where man, in his ignorance, has made it impossible by changing natural conditions. I predict that
before night there will be some parasite at work
among these caterpillars. We'll watch and see.

You know one of the things a good Forester must know is what insects to protect and what ones to exterminate."

"Why, do you ever protect any?" asked Harry, in surprise.

"Oh, yes, indeed. We learned long ago that the most efficacious way to fight insects is with insects."

They were examining a spot that seemed to be especially alive with the crawling things, when Uncle Bob called them over to observe a strange sight he had discovered. There, before them was a long-legged yellow-brown fly that the boys had often seen before but had never paid much attention to. Deftly and quickly the long-legged fellow flew from worm to worm, lighting on each just long enough to force a sort of a stinger into the back of a caterpillar, and then on to the next one.

The boys were amazed, and naturally looked to their uncle for an explanation.

"That is the Ichneuman fly, boys," he said, "and she is very busy stinging and laying her eggs in the segments of the caterpillar. You see she has a great eye for the future. The caterpillar will soon build its chrysalid, expecting in due time to hatch into a moth, but long before that happens the egg of that fly will hatch inside the cocoon and eat the body of the moth-to-be. Its egg-laying propensity is thereby cut off, and the pest dies out.

"That one fly will perhaps sting a thousand caterpillars, and no doubt there are many hundreds of them at work to-day. It is their harvest time. See here! Here is a ground wasp doing substantially the same thing, except that she is carrying the worms away. Let us follow her."

Soon they came to a tiny round hole in the ground. The wasp unceremoniously shoved the worm into the hole, kicked dirt into the cavity with her hind legs, and then started straightway to excavate a second hole close at hand.

"You see, boys, the wasp lights on the worm and injects the poison through its stinging apparatus. That paralyzes the worm. She then lays her eggs in the body and deposits it in the ground. When the young wasps hatch they devour the meat. It is the way of Nature."

The boys learned many such lessons the next couple of weeks while they were waiting for the advance guard to come on to the mill. One day, while cutting underbrush, Harry uncovered a great pile of disintegrated pine cones. He dug about them with his heavy boot, and to his surprise they went into the ground at least three feet, while here and there among them were pockets of green cones that it was very evident had been carefully hidden by some one. He called to

Harvey and together they carefully investigated.

"Squirrels must have done it," said Harry, at length.

"Oh, bosh!" exclaimed Harvey. "All the squirrels in the U. S. A. couldn't pile up pine cones like that. Why, there must be millions of them rotting here together."

After some discussion they gathered up some of the larger cones and worked their way over the ridge to where Mr. Standish was making preparation to erect a high tower for use in watching for fires. As was his custom when the Scouts came to him with a question, he took the necessary time to explain matters to them carefully.

"Yes, squirrels, boys. Probably Douglas squirrels. You see they are up long before you are, and they come together in little parties every morning to eat their breakfast. They cut away the shingles of the cones and remove the dainty nut-seed that is under every scale. When they have finished one cone they dive off into the woods to where they have hidden countless others and bring another. So it goes on, year in and year out, until there is a great pile of shells. These slowly rot away and make fertilizer for the woods. I have seen patches forty to fifty feet square and sometimes three feet deep,—perhaps the accumulation of fifty years.

"The interesting thing to the forester about

it all, though, boys, is that the squirrels never find nearly all the cones they bury. Dirt gets in about them, they sprout, and the first thing you know there is a tiny new tree, and the squirrel has become a forester. Countless millions of trees are thus planted each year by these noisy little folk. True, they do eat a great many of the seed, but in the long run what they so carefully bury makes up for what they eat. That process often explains how it is that young trees sprout so soon on a burned-over area. The cones and seed are already in the ground germinating, and when the sun and rain gets to them they grow rapidly.''

A few days later the Supervisor came again and announced that the advance mill crowd would be along in ten days to clear and set up the mill. That meant just ten days to cruise the valley.

"I'll bring Tompkins and Toney in the morning. You bring the Scouts along, and the cruise books for the section, and we'll get at it. You can take charge, and I will come after the cruisers and mark the trees that are to be cut."

So it was that the next morning found each of the Scouts with a simple pair of calipers, at work in the woods measuring the diameters of the trees, while Tompkins and Toney estimated at a glance how many saw logs sixteen feet long each tree would make.

"Yellow Western, twenty-eight—four," called

Tompkins. Then, "Silver, thirty-one—five," called Toney. Then "Lodge pole, fourteen—four," Tompkins would call, and Uncle Bob hastily made his records, the first number being the diameter of the tree, breast-high, and the second the approximate number of saw logs the tree would make.

The Supervisor came along behind, his Government ax over his shoulder, marking the timber. Here and there he would blaze a great giant pine at its base, and then turning his ax over would deftly stamp into the blaze a bold "U. S." by means of the heavy raised letters on the head of his ax.

Thus it was that the timber of Bald Knob Valley was cruised and marked ready for cutting. Soon the now sublime silence would be broken by the sickening sound of the engine as the hungry saw forced its steel fangs into the resinous wood and flung the sweet-scented sawdust into the air. A majestic growth of perhaps three hundred years would be cut in a few months' time and shipped off to form a part of the busy world's commerce.

That day's work finished in the low wet end of the valley where there had once stood a magnificent forest of yellow pine that had been burned very severely perhaps a hundred and fifty years before. Here tangled through the splendid second growth were countless millions of decaying, rotting logs, laying just where some gale had toppled them over after the flames had made them insecure. Here and there a mighty ghostlike trunk still stood, preserved in its embalming fluid of pure pine pitch. Among those logs the Scouts discovered the most gorgeous fungi they had ever seen. There were toadstools of red and yellow and brown, flat, domed, and cup-shaped, growing in rank profusion.

"Oh, aren't they beautiful!" cried Harvey. "I'd like to gather a whole wagonful just to keep."

"If it wasn't for these," said Tompkins, kindly, "there would be no forests on these mountains at all. They just work away here, quietly but surely, and no one sees their work."

"But what on earth do they do, Tompkins?" asked Harry, eagerly.

"Why, listen," said the Supervisor. "You see this great tangle of down timber, don't you? Every one of those rotting logs was like that magnificent old stub there—hard as flint and as sound as oak. The forest was partially destroyed, and those great logs were cleared away ready for a new growth, but if left alone it would take a hundred years for them to decay even to a semi-rotten state. Why, before they could return to earth again a second calamity might befall this valley and topple over on them a second installment. In a thousand years the forest would be one great enormous pile of rubbish, incapable of any further growth. But Nature is a wise guardian of her domains, and so she gave all these great stretches of waste to the different families of fungi, and in a surprisingly short time they take the largest, hardest trees and reduce them to rot and return them to the soil ready to be used over again by the new growth. With the aid of these brightly colored fellows, twenty years sees the forest comparatively clear and ready for new growth. The fungi are the forest's chambermaids, and they are always busy tidying things up. Now and then a gray squirrel carries one of the largest mushrooms home for a special feast, but on the whole they grow and multiply by the millions and do their good work.''

The next day a temporary camp was set up and the mill crew set to work cutting a road up through a thick growth of lodge pole pine to where the big camp was to set. Pine Cone Camp flourished, and before the week was out the road was opened up and the first loads of the simple mill arrived, then came loads of light-weight rails, funny little flat cars, and a squatty, sneezy engine.

What surprised the boys most of all was the tremendous number of length of smoke stack that were brought in. They were to learn afterward that it was necessary to run a very tall stack to get up above the trees for draft, and second, by so doing there was not near the danger from treacherous sparks.

A huge skeleton of aspens was erected and covered with canvas to serve as stable for the sturdy teams that were to carry lumber out to the railroad. Then came the big mess-tent and kitchen where was to be manufactured the food for a hundred hungry men. The bunk house was a crude frame affair, built largely of poles and the cull lumber of the first few days sawing, roofed over with rolls of heavy asbestos roofing.

The rollways were arranged. The sawdust pit was dug under the saw and arranged so a queer one-horse dump cart could drive right under and get the dust as it accumulated. There were men with pevies and pike poles, there were men with axes and long cross-cut saws. There was a tumbled-together blacksmith shop, where axes and saws were kept in shape, and last, but not least, there was a clearing off to one side where a half board, half tent shack was put up for the residence of the Government inspector. Out at the edge of the clearing rose the majestic forest of Bald Knob Valley—superb timber, one of the country's greatest bits of natural wealth.

The men were all friendly disposed to the Scouts, and in fact it was only a few days until

they had many real friends among the rough hard-
working men, and many were the interesting
yarns and bits of reminiscence they heard, both
at the table and about the camps. True, there
were some that were coarse and made sport of the
young Foresters, and a few who even showed them
contempt. As everywhere else in the world where
there is a large company of men, there was every
kind, and the boys soon learned with whom to be
friendly and whom to avoid.

There was one fellow—a big, rawboned, fierce
looking chap, that was not at all careful of his appearance or his talk, to whom both boys early
took a dislike. One of the men had hinted to
Harvey that this unlikeable fellow was a timber
drifter, who worked at one mill awhile and then
moved on. He had been on the job only a few
days and seemed, for some reason of his own,
to wish to be left absolutely alone. He was a
good workman, however, and could easily beat any
other man in camp with a broad ax. He could
cut and dress three trees while most men were
making one, and he did it with an ease that was
marvelous. He was a woodsman, born to the use
of an ax, and there was no doubting it, he was an
artist. His vocabulary was very meager and
consisted largely of words and terms that are
usually excluded from polite society. He always
had a generous chew of tobacco in his protruding

cheek, and could spit oftener and with more precise accuracy than a squirt-gun.

He eyed the boys closely whenever they came near him, and to both there was sort of an irresistible curiosity about him. Whether it was his utter uncouthness or his semi-wildness that attracted them, they did not know; but very often they found themselves just staring at his huge frame strung with muscles of steel that stood out like whip cords, or at his sad, half-wistful face that was covered with weeks of unkempt whiskers. There was something simply irresistible about his gray eye.

Things were getting pretty well organized. The track was laid up the valley and the steam loaders that were placed along the track were gotten into shape. Attached to each was a large steel drum upon which was wound a fine high tension steel cable. This cable was run out up the valley to where the loggers were getting out the logs. Instead of snaking them in with a team, as in the old-fashioned logging, this cable was simply attached to the log when ready, and with a puff and a snort the dingy little donkey engine would pull it into the track with an ease that was almost comical. To be sure, this dragging process was very hard on the small trees and young seedlings, yet it was a time-saver and therefore a moneymaker, and could do as much work in one day as a dozen teams of the best horses. The cable was released when the log was deposited on the rollway and pulled back into the woods ready for another log by means of a simple back line that was wound on a small drum and a stout pulley fastened to some sturdy tree out in the forest.

Sometimes it would happen that the inrushing log would strike some obstacle, and then with a sudden snarl it would pitch high in the air, turn over perhaps end for end, and then fall a heavy dead weight again in the slash and small trees. Woe to the "cutter" or "rigger" or "sawer" that got in the way of one of these enormous green logs on its resisting way to the saw mill!

Jaycox, for that was the name of the strange wild man of the camp, had never before worked in a camp that employed a steam skidder and was constantly in danger of being crushed, for he had long made it a habit to compel his huge brute strength to save him in an emergency, instead of his small and less active brain.

His turn came in spite of all warning and threats. A great log on its way in, with the irresistible little donkey on one end, struck a stump, flew high in the air, turned on end, made one great half circle, and fell, stripping the heavy limbs out of a great Western and dropping them, in the twinkling of an eye, on Jaycox's mighty form. This was too much for him. His body swayed and then sank to the ground under the mass of débris.

He was quickly rescued and hurried to the mill, but it was very evident his spine was hurt and that one shoulder was crippled. The foreman, a sturdy Dutchman, was quite put out, for he prided himself on the few accidents there were in his camps. He was a boss who had a man for everything, and everything assigned to a man, and when every man held up his end, accidents were wellnigh impossible.

He had been afraid from the first that Jaycox would get killed, for it was very evident the man, if he had brains, rarely ever used them. He seemed to be entirely preoccupied all the while and his work was merely mechanical.

At the mill it was decided to take him to the Forester's cabin, for, as the foreman said:

"Mrs. Standish is worth all the doctors in the State of Colorado to a hurt lumberman. Why, anybody would get well with her a'fussing over them."

Jaycox objected with all the strength he had. He had no use for women of any kind or description and declared he would rather die in the camp than go to the cabin. However, it was decided best for him, and he was placed on a stretcher and hurried away, while the great circular saw groaned on and while the stubborn little donkey engines yanked countless logs to the rollways.

It was just before noon when they arrived. "Courageous" lay in his customary place in the sun. High was dozing in his big chair, and Aunt Belle was singing merrily at her work. The rustic gate swung open with a squeak. Harry had come with the injured man and so now led the little procession.

"Courageous" came to life like a flash and made a violent lunge to get away, his nose high to the wind. Harry spoke to him several times, but to no avail. As the party drew nearer the house the bear made such a commotion that High awoke with a start and sat up, while Aunt Belle hurried out to see what could be wrong.

"Courageous" was wild. He pawed the air, he whined piteously, he lurched out to the end of his chain with enough force to break it, only to be flung flat by the taut chain. He rose to his hind legs, whiffed violently, and then gave one last terrific lurch. The chain gave way at the collar and "Courageous" was free. He trembled a moment and then, without so much as a glance backward, he made for the timber and was gone as if pursued by all the evil spirits in creation. Evidently he had smelled the odor that told him of slaughter, of struggle, of a cold, lifeless, bloody mother that could not feed her children. He had smelled a man smell that was associated with all that was terrible in his young bear life, and he was gone.

The little cavalcade pressed on to the shade of the porch, where the injured man was placed on an old settle until other arrangements could be made for him inside. Jaycox's tired gray eye met High's. There was a flash in both, but neither man spoke. The men withdrew at the suggestion of Mrs. Standish, all save Harry, and he lingered. He hastened to bring fresh water from the spring, and when well out of ear shot, Jaycox turned wearily on his couch and whispered across to High:

" 'Remember Pete Swanson!' I see you recognize me. Sheepmen are always loyal to each other. I had sworn to get Jacobus, and I did. The old score is clean now, all but one. I'll get Hastings soon. He should not have meddled with my father."

"But they are free," said High, in an unguarded moment. "They broke jail."

A fierce light of joy sprang into Jaycox's eyes, and he continued:

"Swear you will not betray me!"

"Only on one condition," hissed High.

"What?" demanded Jaycox.

"That you leave the country in thirty days, and that you agree not to in the slightest way harm the Service. They saved my life."

"I agree," said Jaycox, hesitatingly.

"A sheepman's word is honor," replied High.

"Give me a chance to join my father and we will strike for Montana," said Jaycox. "Are they hunting him with a posse?"

"Yes, the Sheriff is—"

"If they catch him, I will have one or two more to get before I go, for when I go Luke goes with me. I came all the way from Montana, horseback, to clean up my score and get Dad and the kid. I have a sheep ranch there."

Mrs. Standish interrupted further talk by entering to doctor the injured man. A few days of careful nursing, hot applications and rest, soon put Jaycox back on his feet and he was back at the mill doing light work about the engine.

He had just emerged from the sawdust pit as Harry came down the trail. Like a flash an idea came into Harry's mind. He had been turning a fancy over in his mind ever since the day of the accident, and with the sudden appearance of Jaycox the fancy seemed to take shape. There was most certainly some strange connection between this Jaycox and "Courageous," of that he was certain, but in just what way, he had not been able to determine. It came home like a flash. That cub had smelled Jaycox before and had a decided dislike for him. "Why—why—why then, he must have been the man that shot and skinned his mother!'' he breathed. As he thought about this discovery, many things seemed to straighten out in his mind. Jaycox must have been the camper on the mountain where the stolen canned goods were. If so, it was he that had burned them out. The bear's hide was found at High's cabin, to be sure, yet ''Courageous'' was very fond of High. Evidently the hated man-smell was not on old High Tucker but on Jaycox.

''Oh, then I have my desperado!'' cried Harry, ''—all but to catch him; and then I can clear Old High of every bit of suspicion. But first, I must get more evidence. I'll talk to High at once. No, I'll keep it all a secret till I'm sure. I'll watch him closely every day and plan a way to capture him.''

CHAPTER VIII

"FIRES! fires! fires!" said Mr. Standish, wearily. "We have never had so many before, and I suppose it is the dry season and so many careless saw mill hands. Yet, sometimes, I think Luke is at the bottom of most of them. I wish he could be captured.

"It was only yesterday Toney succeeded in putting out what in an hour's time would have been a terrific fire by riding hard and then beating out the flames with his wet saddle blanket. If a bit of a breeze had arisen we would have had Famine Valley aflame in no time. Toney is one of the wisest fire-fighters in the Service, and it seems to me that the Supervisor would do well to put him over at the mill, at least until we have rain, for those miserable little 'donkies' kick sparks into the air like every day was the Fourth of July."

"Mr. Kable is very watchful, though, Uncle," reassured Harry. "He has the entire camp organized in squads, each squad with a leader, and every man knows just what he's to do in case of trouble. They have shovels a-plenty, and extra axes, saws, plows, and rakes. Then he keeps

174

three good teams in the coral all the time for fear they will need them. There is dynamite in the supply shed, and at every donkey engine and loader there are several barrels of water. The men are forbidden to smoke while at work in the woods, and everywhere about the camp are 'Safety First' signs tacked up. I noticed that everywhere it can be put is a warning of some kind.

"Even on the little packages of matches the men carry is a little saying about how one tree will make a million matches but one match can destroy a million trees. Some of the men have pocket whet stones with a warning printed on them, and in the bottom of every tin cup at the mess table is printed a 'Safety First' idea about fires. The men get it drilled into them morning, noon, and night, until it is a part of them."

"Kable is a wise man," replied Mr. Standish, thoughtfully. "We need many, many more such mill bosses. If we had them we wouldn't have so many catastrophes. Just think, lads,—sixteen hundred fires in Idaho last year with a loss of over three hundred million feet of lumber. It isn't only the lumber loss, though, that is important. Just think of the money it takes out of circulation, of the men it throws out of work, of the lives it endangers, and of the way it devastates the land. It takes a hundred years for burned areas to get on their feet again."

slept w
sounds,
my us
came t
six of
keep t
for fe
bunch
They
the he
that l
part
Utah,
memb
"O
next y
nearly
etern
shoul
that l
credi
But t
"A
my o
bush.
been
pecti
open
ized

force-pump
to extinguish
out from under

control. It was very unusual that they had no
rain, for notwithstanding two or three mountain
showers there had been no real rainfall for weeks
and the whole country was beginning to show it.

"Here come the Question Boxes!" laughingly
spoke the foreman at the mill. "Those boys know
more about the 'ifs' and 'ands' of this lumber
business now than a lot of these hands that have
been doing nothing else all their lives. They just
naturally want to know everything,—from what
makes an apparently sound log hollow in the mid-
dle, to what caused one place to be hard and another place soft in the same tree."

"Hello, Bill!" called the Scouts, as they came to
the mill. "Say, what makes some of those big
logs just check up at the center until they damage
all the lumber, while others rot out at the center
completely?"

The head saw-master laughed as he spat on the
ground, a merry twinkle in his eye.

"You got me, kids, completely. Why does your
mother keep pigs?" replied the foreman.

"We'll find out, you bet," said Harry, friendly-
like. "I'll bet Mr. Kable will know, and if he
doesn't Old High will."

"Old High who?" questioned the mill man.

"Old High Tucker, a friend of the Supervisor's," replied Harry.

"So Old High's over there, is he? Well, I'll

be derned! So that's where they have been hiding him. Trying to save him from that nosey Sheriff, eh! Well, he'll get him yet. I'll bet a donkey engine, cable and all. He's the crazy old duffer that shot up Jacobus some little time ago, ain't he!''

"No, sir, he isn't the man," said Harry, stoutly. "It was some one else."

"I don't suppose you know nothing about it," continued the mill hand, kindly. "It was just another verse to a long-standing scrap, I believe, and who can tell but what old Jacobus had it coming to him. Is Old High and this Luke something-or-other the same old duffer?—Been a regular bad actor in his day, so I've been told. Some one was telling me the other night he could cut and trim to perfection more trees in a day than any man that had ever been seen on the range."

"More than Jaycox, even!" questioned Harvey.

"Yes, even more than Jay, and he's some wonder. Say, did you ever see him dress a log! He goes at it like he just had exactly sixteen seconds to live by the alarm clock and had to cut all the rest of the trees in the world before the crack of doom. He's a rip-snorter, there's no getting around it—a regular ring-tailed lallapalooza, but he ain't in it with this Old High Luke you speak of, leastways if you can believe what you hear."

"But High and Luke are two different men," carefully explained Harry. "Luke was the tie-

cutter, but Old High is a prospector and ex-Forest
Ranger. He was badly hurt in an auto accident.
That's why he is at the cabin. You are mistaken
about him, sir. He is as fine an old man as you
ever met, and the Sheriff doesn't want him. It's
just Old Luke's remaining boy that he is after.
Would you know him if you'd see him? We must
be going now. Got to keep our eyes open for fires
mighty closely these days. Wish it would rain
about a week, don't you?"

"Rain! With that pile of logs there to be
sawed?" questioned the mill man. "Why, I
should say not. Don't want a drop until the last
log on the job is turned to lumber and saw dust,
then let her come 'pitch-forks and nigger-babies'
as we used to say when I was a kid; but rain now?
—no!"

"Logs, logs," said Harvey, as he let his gaze
wander. "Why, it seems to me there are enough
cut and piled up here now to run the country a
year, and yet there are hundreds of mills, you
said, bigger than this one, cutting and cutting.
What is going to become of these timber lands in
a few years?"

"Logs is right, boy; logs, and then some more.
Say, did you know that if all the logs that are cut
in this U. S. A. for one year should be piled on a
trans-continental road in piles one hundred feet
high they'd reach from New York City to Frisco?

—Did you? And listen, boy, it takes careful cutting from a million acres annually to supply the
railroads poles and ties alone. Pooh! all we cut
here all Fall wouldn't make a drop in the bucket.
The world needs logs and plenty of them. I
ain't a'worrying about what's going to happen to
them all. There's plenty for *now*, and let the next
generation get out and hatch up some substitutes.''

"Yes, but that isn't conservation," replied
Harry, indignantly. "What if they don't find
suitable substitutes—what then? That is why
there is a National Forest Service. That is why
owners of great private tracts are employing
foresters—to look out for the future, to fight loss
and waste and insects and fires and ignorance.
Why, trees are a crop, just like wheat and potatoes, only they don't ripen every year, only every
hundred and fifty. I tell you, if I were Uncle
Sam, you mill men couldn't do as you are doing
here on this cut—killing millions of young trees
and littering up the fields simply awful. Why, the
way you get out logs is like peeling an apple with
the peelings an inch thick. Down in the cities
folks pay enormous prices for wood, and here
are millions of tons of it going to waste, no good
to any one. You wouldn't even stop to make ties
from the tops if the law didn't compel you to.
Why, there are seven thousand ties piled in the

clearing now, ready for shipment, and there will be that many more.''

''You are too scientific for me,'' said the saw master, as he again turned to his work.

The boys moved up the track and were soon in the heart of the cutting district. They paused to watch two powerful ''fellers'' as they rested on their ax-handles a moment. They were cutting the notch in a giant yellow pine, preparatory to felling the great tree with their saw.

''I wonder if they can always make them fall just where they want them to?'' asked Harry.

''I suppose not,'' said Harvey. ''Let's ask them how they work it.''

In a second the question was put, and the cutters were glad to pause a moment and visit before beginning the tremendous exertion of sawing the great ''veteran.''

''Put 'em just where we please, boys,'' said the one, jokingly. ''Stand over yonder and we'll fell this one right behind your ear like a big lead pencil.''

''No, thanks!'' said Harry, merrily. ''But I think it is wonderful if you are able to put them where you want to. Won't you explain it to us how you do it?''

''Simple!'' replied the first man. ''It's all in the notch. I can stick a stake in the ground and drive it out of sight with a falling trunk, any day.

I'll prove it to you." So taking his ax he cut a stout stake, stepped back fifty or sixty feet, carefully surveyed the notch that they had been making, and then started the stake in the soft forest floor with his ax.

The sawing began, the sharp ribbon of steel eating its way into the soft wood as if by magic. The boys were ordered to step back to a safe distance, and before they realized it the great trunk gently vibrated, then tipped slightly in the direction of the notch, then with a mighty swish and cracking of brittle branches the monarch fell, striking the stake squarely on the head and forcing it out of sight in the dirt.

"Great!" cried the boys. "You men are artists for sure! But it makes me sick to see those big trees fall and be dragged about by a steel cable, just as if they were dead poles. I'll bet that one was three hundred years old—just think of it! Older than Uncle Sam. And now all it's good for is a few boards."

"Don't you think it!" laughed one of the cutters. It's good for flooring, and plank, and bridge timbers, and ship beams, and flag poles, and wagon beds, and car frames, and houses, and—and—oh, almost anything you can think of, boys. This whole blooming civilization we boast so much about is based and founded on trees like this one. They are what make the world go round. They are what Progress eat. So get rid of your cheap sentiment. If we did as some of these city chaps want us to, we would put all these great trees in a greenhouse and save 'em for party decorations. Trees make commerce, commerce makes money, and money is what makes the mare go. So get ep, Napoleon! It looks like rain and we have six or eight more such slivers to fell yet before that feed gong rattles." The men were gathering their tools together to move on.

"Let's count the annual rings," said Harvey, "and see for ourselves. I'll bet this tree is older than Jerusalem."

"Not so bad as that, but let's see."

Soon they were busy counting with the point of their Scout knives.

"Five hundred and eighty-one," said Harry in great admiration. "What babies we are yet! All the grave stone this old fellow will ever get is that mammoth stump."

They circled the great slash piles, came down past where the donkey engines were tugging out their hearts on logs or lifting them to flat cars, then on past the great piles of ties where they were being stamped and pulled away with teams of horses; on around the enormous slab piles, and back to the great lumber stacks, the bunk house and little office.

Just as they reached the road leading to the

mill office, a gray-haired, wind-bronzed man, who sat his nervous mountain pony with perfect grace and ease, galloped by the lane, pulled in his reins, and hailed the boys.

"Howdy, lads. Where is Mr. Kable, can you tell me?"

The boys both noted with interest the star he wore on his vest and knew at once they were talking to the County Sheriff.

"Yes, sir. He is out yonder on this side of the slab pile."

The Sheriff wheeled his pony in the direction indicated, and was gone.

At that moment Jaycox rounded the end of the slab pile, ax in hand, caught sight of the rider, and instantly turned his back toward him, bent over, and began to chop, keeping one eye on the Sheriff without appearing to see him.

The Sheriff pulled up directly in front of him. "I'm looking for Kable, my friend. Where is he?"

"Other side of the pile," said Jaycox, pointing with his thumb, "or at the office. I'll call him for you."

"Needn't mind, thank you. I'll locate him." And he rode on.

He had hardly rounded the slab pile when Jaycox became as alert as a squirrel. He climbed the pile and peered cautiously over. He could not see, but he could hear, and what he heard so interested him that he deliberately stretched out flat on the pile and lay with his hand to his ear.

"Howdy! Kable. Great weather for a saw mill, eh? How much more are you going to cut in old Bald Knob? Great logs, those."

"Yes, Taylor, great; and things are moving so nicely we have made application for another five million feet. It's here easily, and is ripe. It ought to be cut. That will run us clear into winter. Wish it would rain, though. Those confounded slash piles are getting too big to suit me. If it would ever get afire in a wind it would wipe us out like flees."

"So it would; so it would," said the Sheriff, absentmindedly.

"So it would!" sneered Jaycox from his hiding place, "and—and—by the eternal gods, so it shall, if you are going to have such visitors often. That duffer is always butting in. He's after me."

"Got a bit of business with you yourself, Kable."

"That so?— Want to build a new jail, or something, Taylor? Can sell you a lot of choice culls cheap just now."

"Haw! haw! May need a new jail before I get through if it keeps on. I've got the old calaboose full now, tight, and all bad eggs, every one. But you see, as a matter of fact, I'm after a few more.

We sheriffs are never satisfied. Yew see it's like this a'way. A little bird, with much tobacco spitting and a regular flood of cursing, informs me that the very man I want is in your camp."

Jaycox's jaws tightened. "High has squealed on me!" he hissed. "Who else would know it?—Don't suppose those Scout kids are next! I'll—"

"In my camp, eh? Well, that's strange. You know blamed well, Taylor, I'd never hire a crook if I knowed it. But this time you are just naturally mistaken. I've had all these hands some time. Haven't hired a new one since the mill was moved in."

"That so? Well, course I may have gotten on a fake trail. I've thought I knew where my man was for some time, but Standish declares I'm plumb off, that I must look again. His judgment is true as an automatic, too. I'm looking for Luke's eldest boy. He is somewhere in these parts; has been recognized a time or two."

"Old Luke's kid!" cried Kable sternly. "Taylor, you forget I am a cowman. You don't think I'd ever hire a sheepman, do you? Not if I knew it, anyway."

"Never thought of that, Kable," returned the Sheriff thoughtfully. "But perhaps he's here under an assumed name of some kind."

"Well, if he is, you are welcome to him, Taylor, that's sure. All you got to do is to find him."

Jaycox's face was distorted with hatred and his mighty shoulders worked nervously. "So you are a cattle man, are you?" he breathed. "Well, so much more the reason why I should get you. I'll beat you at your little game, gents, both of you. Lord! what a fire she'll make!" But he was interrupted here by the conversation at the other side of the pile.

"How do you propose to prove he's here, Taylor?"

"I want to stick around for supper and take a look. I believe I could identify the rascal if he's here."

"You're more than welcome. Stay a week if you like, if you can stand our diet."

"Say, Kable, you check your men at supper and see if they are all there. If my man is here, my presence in the camp may make him suspicious and he may lay out till I'm gone."

"A wise precaution, Taylor. I'll divide them into their fire squads after mess and they can be checked up that way."

"Good! Now I'll take a little look around." He turned and rode up the trail to where the men were rolling logs from the flat cars to the rollways.

Jaycox noted with satisfaction that Kable went into the office. He rose to get down, just as Harry came out of the woods, and, because this same Jaycox had warned him only a day before to stay off the slab piles because it was dangerous, he wondered what the man could be doing there now himself. As he watched him he suddenly became aware that the pile was falling, and he broke into a run. He found Jaycox spilled on the ground, cursing the air blue, while blood gushed from his nose. The pile had slipped and pitched the man on his face in the gravel. Already his one eye was swelling shut and his lip swelling where his big front teeth had cut into it.

"Don't tell 'em what happened, kid," he growled. "They'd give me the 'horse' for a month. I ought to have known better. Tell 'em a log knocked me over."

At mess the boss ordered the fire gangs together, and then took occasion to tell them once more of the increasing danger from fire, and urged them to hold themselves in readiness for any call, adding that some difficulty had arisen at the railroad and they were going to hold their lumber for a better price, so the extra need for special care.

The Sheriff moved about from group to group, but found nothing that gave him a clew, and just as the men began to gather about the big circle where they usually sat about a fire to smoke and tell stories, he rode away into the darkness. Jaycox watched them go, and then withdrew, supposedly to bathe his bruised countenance but in reality to think out his plan, for it was very evident things were getting hot for him.

The next day the Supervisor made a personal visit to the mill to see for himself about fire conditions, and before he left that night he decided it expedient to stretch a telephone line from well back in the cutting area to Mr. Standish's cabin and from there to join the main line to headquarters.

"It may save hours, in case of trouble," he said, "and with that enormous slash and slab pile I want to be ready for any emergency. If it does not rain soon the whole forest belt is going to be burned over. Hundreds of fires are now raging in the Sierras; whole towns have burned out in Wisconsin; Minnesota and Michigan have great tracts aflame, and every day we get more reports. The whole forest floor is as dry as tinder and as inflammable as powder. Kable, you ought to keep a night guard until it showers."

"Can't sit up all night and work all day, Hastings, but I'll do all that lies in my power."

The next day Harry and Harvey were summoned to help stretch a simple line through the valley over the ridges to Mr. Standish's cabin, where it was hooked into the main line. Toney climbed the trees and cut the tops out of them, while Tompkins came after him, nailed on the insulators, and the boys helped work out the wire and aided the men in general.

"Say, Scouts, you should have been with me yesterday," said Toney.

The boys looked interested.

"Tell us about it, Toney. You didn't see 'Courageous,' did you?"

"No. No such luck, boys, but I know you would have enjoyed being with me."

"What were you doing, Toney?" pled Harry.

"I was planting spawn in all the headwaters on our watershed—millions of them."

"Planting spawn?" said both boys.

"Yes, greenhorns!—Putting young trout in the streams. They were really fingerlings. I put two cans in East Beaver, two in Grass Valley, two in Little Fountain, one in Famine Creek, and four in Rock Creek."

"Why, do Foresters take care of the fishing, too?" asked Harry in astonishment.

"Yes, always," replied Toney. "We plant millions of them every season and in that way keep the streams stocked. In three years they will be 'frys' and ready for us to eat. They come from the State Fish Hatcheries and are supplied free for any stream that does not cross private property. All of these little streams teem with Uncle Sam's trout cared for by the Foresters."

"And you care for birds, and protect game, and plant fish, and fight insects! Oh, my! Oh, my! I used to think a Forest Ranger was a sort of a hero that rode about all day just having a good time. I didn't know he cruised timber, built trails, sold logs, fought beetles, burned brush, and a million other things. I think it's great. I want to do it all my life. I'm going to be a Forester, I tell you, and I want to be the very best and wisest kind of a one."

"Here, too," chimed in Harvey. "I want to be a Supervisor on a mountain forest."

"Uncle Bob calls this sort of thing going to school," chuckled Harvey. "I wish I didn't ever have to go back to the other kind. But of course I must. A fellow has to go to school to amount to anything."

It was full moon, and the clear, cool nights in the forest were wonderful to the boys. Even the tired woodsmen responded and lingered longer than was their wont about the little friendly fire, spinning yarns and taking in the rugged beauties of the night, one yarn leading to another.

"This season would be a dandy for the old timber pirates of a dozen years ago," said one.

"You bet!" said another. "There never was a slash pile in better shape for dirty work than that one of ours yonder."

"Good thing Peg-leg Jones hung long ago,"

said another, "or he'd be looking for just such a chance."

"Who was Peg-leg Jones?" begged Harry, who was just aching for a real yarn.

"Peg-leg Jones!" replied the cutter in astonishment. "Didn't you ever hear of Peg-leg? He was the slickest timber pirate the West has ever had."

"Tell us about him, please," begged Harvey.

"Well, there really isn't much to tell, lad. He was an old duffer with a wooden leg and set some of the worst forest fires the West has ever seen. I mind the last one he set—burned at least three hundred thousand acres clean of the finest timber in the world."

"How did he do it without being caught?" asked Harry eagerly.

"Easiest thing in the dictionary, lad. He'd arrange a bit of slash just right so as to be sure to get his fire started on a good, dry floor, then he would set a burning glass so's the sun would focus itself through it and light the little pile of needles; but long before the sun got around Peg-leg would be far away, making certain folks see him in a saloon or game parlor, so he could always prove an alibi. I suppose he'd be doing that little game yet if it hadn't a'been for his jaw."

"Why, what did his jaw have to do with it?" asked Harry innocently.

"Oh, that's easy," laughed the cutter. "When he was off on one of his alibi trips once't he got drunk and happy, and his jaw up and told a lot of onlookers all about his little game. When Pegleg came to,—that is, sobered enough to be himself,—he found himself out under a spreading Yellow Western about to be strung up. He pled awful hard for a chance, but he had done so much dirt with his fires that they just naturally couldn't resist punishing him."

"Snake Trotter's game was a better one," suggested an engineer.

"How was that?" came from a dozen interested voices. Jaycox had joined the crowd now and sat listening.

"Snake did the same sort of dirty work, only he used long-time fuse and powder. Set his fires in old, hollow, pitch-soaked logs and then left them. Sometimes it would take his fuse twelve hours to burn to the powder, and he would be fifty miles away when she lighted up. He used to use his little game to burn over forest for his sheep, and it worked, too. No one would ever have suspected Snake if he hadn't been the heir of bad luck and got blowed to pieces once."

"How was that, Jim?" queried another one of the circle. "I have often heard of Snake Trotter's fires but never did know what sort of an end he came to."

"Well, it seemed he planned a big fire and had everything set for it,—had a choice old pine hollow. But some prospector beat him to it and had used the hollow tree for a storehouse to keep his supply of dynamite in. Snake lit his longtime fuse and left. Nothing happened. So, after a few days, he went back to investigate. He discovered his fuse had gone out and that the tree was loaded full of dynamite. He was delighted, and was busy re-setting his machine, using the dynamite as a scatterer, when the prospector shows up, and not knowing what Snake was up to he took a shot at him, hit the dynamite, and—and now Snake is fertilizing the surrounding country. He left sudden't and he hain't come back."

The men laughed in great good humor, all save Jaycox, and he was lost in thought. A great inspiration had by some means found its way into his brain. He would do as Snake Trotter had done, only he wouldn't use the dynamite.

The next day was Sunday. Jaycox borrowed a horse from Kable to ride to town to consult a doctor about his sore eye, but in reality he went straight to High's cabin on the mountain, secured a generous supply of mine fuse, a new box of dynamite caps, a pair of pinchers to attach them to the fuse, and came back again with a small bottle of creek water from "Dr. Somebody" for his damaged eye. So far his plan was safe.

He carefully hid the fuse in his bunk and then began to formulate his plans. He would begin stealing a little grub supply for future use—for use after the mill and land was black with desolation! He would bury it in the great pile of sawdust of which he was in charge. No fire would ever burn it out save over the top. When all was destroyed he would build a little shelter well hidden in the tangle of burnt and blackened logs, remove his food there, and then go on a still hunt for the Sheriff. It all seemed possible. He could bring it to pass, and he knew it. The great pile of dry pitch slabs was the vulnerable point at the mill, and he could manage that. He would fire them, and he would wait until the wind blew hard. It had blown a good deal of late. His fuses and powder planted once, he could then wait for the proper condition before lighting them. He must not fail, for a fool would know the fire had been set, and if he dared bungle he would certainly be caught.

Still no rain, and still more slash. Every day the Supervisor called to see if all was well. Every day the boys filled every water barrel, piled what brush they could together, and gathered all trash, such as papers, from the valley. Very often Kable investigated the tools, the force-pumps and the other equipment. He wasn't sleeping well. He was getting nervous. The

strain was telling on him. Daily came reports of
awful devastations in the timber lands farther to
the west of them. Every paper that reached the
isolated camp was filled with wild headlines of
"Fire! Fire! Fire!"

Jaycox laid his plans carefully and well. His
store of groceries had gotten to be quite sufficient
for his stay, so he thought. He carefully hid a
shovel and sharp ax in his sawdust cave. He borrowed all the matches he dared without arousing
suspicion. Next came High's old gun that he had
hung high in a tree before asking for employment
at the new mill of Kable. He had but six rounds
of ammunition for it, and it must be saved for self-
defense only, or for the Sheriff. So he carefully
removed the gun and shells from their hiding and
placed them along with his other treasures in the
sawdust.

Next he arranged his fuses and powder in the
slab pile as occasion allowed, taking care to place
next the fire only pitch-saturated slabs that would
light easily, and once lighted would burn fiercely.
Next came the fuses in the slash piles. The boys
noticed him burying something in the slash, and
when they questioned him about it he remarked,
tersely, that he was fixing to trap a skunk.

"Are there many around? We haven't seen
one yet," said Harry.

"You know the day you saw me on the slab

pile!'' questioned Jaycox, with a leer. ''Well, I was watching two of the biggest skunks I've ever seen that day. They were visiting over behind the slab pile. I'll get 'em both one of these days.'' But his real meaning was entirely lost on the Scouts.

The last arrangement was made, and still no rain. In fact, a hot breeze had been blowing for several days, and Tompkins, Toney, Uncle Bob, and every man they could persuade to work, were busy caring for the little fires all over the Reserve. Every camper, of which there were many, because of the warm, dry weather, was watched carefully and urged to take every precaution. No one anywhere—settlers, miners, or campers, were allowed to build open fires without first getting a permit.

The Supervisor was stern, positive, and determined. Toney, Tompkins, and Uncle Bob were tired, almost to the breaking point, and sore in foot, limb, and arm.

High sat impatiently on the porch of the cabin, unable to take a hand, dreaming big dreams and turning strange thoughts in his mind. Three times the Sheriff had come to him, and by one way or another tried to induce him to talk, but he had remembered Tompkins' advice and kept still. Soon he would be well, and often he wondered if there would be any opposition to his going back to his mine. He must ask Bob Standish at his first opportunity.

The boys were home for dinner the following Sunday, and in spite of Aunt Belle's efforts the talk would go back to forest fires.

"We're all right, and reasonably safe as long as we get no high winds," Tompkins was saying, "for a fire's real destructive power depends on the wind. They can't ever travel against it except in going up a steep hill, and then it isn't likely to do much damage. But what bothers me most is that the prevailing winds are from the slash piles toward the mill. I tell you, boys, if that great dry pile of skeletons ever gets afire in a high wind, nothing on this earth—not all we know about fighting fires—will avail. That entire camp will be cleaned out clean."

"In fighting fires, then," said Harry, "the very first thing to take into consideration is the wind?"

"Correct," replied Uncle Bob; "and not only at the start but all the time. I have known the wind a number of times to completely change during a fire and drive the intense heat and smoke suddenly down upon the fire-fighters, nearly suffocating them. Of course, when it does so it invariably burns itself out, and that is some reward.

"Three things to remember, boys, constantly: The best time to fight a fire is at the beginning. A delay of even a very few minutes may make it impossible to win, for a forest fire in a fair wind gathers headway very rapidly and becomes a raging beast.

"If the ground is thickly covered with leaves and needles, the fire will probably be a ground fire and not burn very fast. Get ahead of it and rake a strip clean of dry material, raking it back to the fire. The best tool for such a job is a four-tined pitch fork. If loose ground or sand is available, it is excellent to spread a strip of it along in front of the fire.

"If the fire is in timber where there are dead trees and slash, it will nearly always change to a top fire. That's when the foliage, dead limbs and dry bark burn. These are hard to fight and very uncertain, for they usually burn on the forest floor too. The most effective way to fight them is by back-firing. Of course a rain or change of wind may come to your rescue, but you can't count on them.

"A back-fire is made by starting another fire some distance ahead of the principal one. The back-fire must be allowed to burn only against the wind and toward the main fire, so that when the two meet they will burn out. To prevent a back-fire from moving with the wind, it should always be started on the windward side of a road or raked strip, or some other natural barrier.

"I'm glad Kable has kept the mill ground

cleared up well, and even in case of a slash fire, with the stream at hand, and if fire could be kept out of that slab pile, the mill and camp might be saved. I'll be the happiest man alive when that will is gone and we once get that slash cared for. Whatever you do, boys, keep your head and don't let so much fire talk get on your nerves. I don't believe we are going to have any trouble at all, for Kable is a wise and careful man and a good leader."

Three days later Kable was called to the city on business. He was loath to leave, but Bob agreed to keep close until he should get back, and so he left easier.

The second day it clouded and looked more like rain than it had for months. There was much thunder and lightning, and everybody fully expected to see a heavy shower, and oh, what a relief it would bring to the parched air and ground. The stream had gotten so low a dam had to be built in order to insure water for engines and table use.

At supper time the wind was blowing a good, stiff breeze, and the entire camp went to bed early, confident of a real rain. However, about midnight the clouds broke, the stars came out faintly and the storm clouds melted. Not so the wind, however. For hours Jaycox had lain awake—watchful, waiting. His bunk was still in the end of the engine house, where it had been put when he had been hurt and he had been changed to night fireman duty.

He arose, dressed himself, went to the door and cautiously peered out. All was still. A second later he was swallowed up in the long, black shadows of the slab pile. Then he skitted like a rabbit from point to point, staying only long enough to make sure the fire was lit, and then finally, wild with excitement, his powerful muscles quivering, he slipped back, hurriedly undressed and climbed into his bunk.

CHAPTER IX

A SEA OF FLAME

"**S**HE'LL burn like a dry prairie to-night!" said Jaycox, half aloud, to himself, as he tried to settle down and patiently wait for the fury he had created.

With the breaking of the clouds the wind had increased noticeably and it had grown colder. Far to the south the sharp lightning cracked and the long, heavy peals of thunder echoed and re-echoed among the hills, like a mighty hidden tom-tom. The fly on the canvas cook-tent flapped a steady and violent tattoo. The rambling bunk-house vibrated in the wind. The double guy wires of the high smokestack sang a weird rattling song as the wind clanged the two taut strands together with every fresh gust.

Both Scouts stirred uneasily. Their sleep was not sound, yet, because they were so entirely weary from the strenuous day in the slash, they slept on.

To Jaycox, seconds seemed hours as he waited impatiently for some alarm that would justify his dressing and getting out into the open. At last he sat erect in bed and whiffed the air as eagerly as a mother deer whiffs it for danger before ven-

turing out. Evidently he was satisfied, for unmistakably he smelled the pungent smoke of burning pine slash.

"She burns!" he breathed again, with great
relief. He then pulled his rough blanket over his
head as if to hide himself from an imaginary re-
proving forest about to be consumed by a fiendish
gale. He could see already in his mind's eye the
awful desolation—acres upon acres of mighty
blackened trunks standing where they had per-
ished. He already imagined the entire slash pile
one glimmering, glowing sheet of flame with a
veritable milky-way of hungry sparks being driven
into new territory by the gale. He could even
now hear the fire front as it went roaring through
the thick second growth of lodge pole just up the
valley.

There was a savage leer on his face as he lay
there entertained by a thousand wild imaginings
—waiting, waiting for some alarm to be sounded.
He felt certain that if it didn't come soon he
would be compelled to flee into the woods for action, for every nerve and every muscle was afire
and demanding expression. He had not long to
wait, for just then a fresh gale swirled down the
clearing and caught the smoke stack squarely.
A pair of guy wires that had rubbed and rubbed on
their anchor unnoticed, snapped. The tall, sooty
pipe leaned slightly toward the bunk-house and

then suddenly hurled itself headlong across the
roof of the squatted building with a terrific rattle, that sounded to the rudely awakened lumber-
jacks like the world had suddenly crashed to
pieces. With many a savage curse they sprang
out of bed, wild eyed and excited, to determine
from which quarter came the disturbance and to
severely punish the offender.

The night was red, the air was foul with pine
smoke, the wind was cold, while tattered yellow
flames rolled and tumbled everywhere.

"Fire!" cried the first man to reach the door.
"Fire!" called the man behind him, and in a
second the wild cry was heard through the camp.

Harry awoke with a start. Was he dreaming?
—"Fire! Fire! The slash's a-fire!" he heard,
and without realizing how he got there he was at
the door of his crude shanty, shivering in the
cold. The heavens were completely filled with a
riot of flame and smoke, while ashes were falling
like snow. Harvey stood at his side now, terri-
fied, with a heavy depressing feeling about his
heart. The slash he had watched so carefully day
in and day out was afire. He had failed again,
and he had been so careful. A great sob broke
from his lips as he stared at the rolling clouds of
gray-green smoke. He saw the men pouring from
the bunk-house, half clad, with their remaining
clothes under their arms. He heard wild shouts

and disjointed orders coming from everywhere. He realized for the first time that Mr. Kable was gone—the great, fearful fire had come, and they had no leader of authority!

In a second both boys were hurrying into their simple clothing. They said not a word until Harry started for the office.

"Where are you going?" cried Harvey.

"To the office to telephone"—and he was gone.

In vain he tried to arouse some one at the Standish cabin. It was useless. Finally it dawned upon him that the instrument was dead. Harvey entered and demanded why he was staying so long.

"Wire's dead!" was the reply.

"Course," said Harvey, laconically. "The stack blew down and snapped the wires just outside the office. I knew that three minutes ago."

"What shall we do? It's one o'clock."

"It's just three miles to Uncle Bob's," said Harvey. "One of us has got to go afoot. The gangs are getting organized, the teams are already hitched, the men have two pumps going on the lumber, but they need a leader out in the timber. I suppose the saw master can boss the mill and lumber yards all right, but what about that fire when it gets onto the Reserve? Who is going to say when to get the back-fires up the valley started? Oh, for Uncle Bob!".

"I'll go!" cried Harry. "I can make it in twenty minutes." He darted through the door and was off, his eager body alert in every nerve. It was now that the Scout pace stood him in good stead. He settled into it easily, and while he was making excellent time over the needle-strewn trail, he was at the same time saving his best for the last stretch or for an emergency. Slowly he climbed the ridge. Once at the top, the rest would be easy. His body was in perfect trim, his muscles, while not large, were wiry, and there was not an ounce of superfluous flesh on his body. The altitude made some difference to his endurance, of course, but at least in part this was overcome by his absorbing eagerness to make time.

At the summit where the trail crossed over the range he paused just a second to look back into Bald Knob Valley. The sight that met his eyes was in that instant stamped on his memory in an indelible fashion. He was sure that to his dying day he could close his eyes and see that wonderful scene just as vividly as he saw it then. Massive, magnificent smoke clouds rose and floated away in the darkness, tinged with every delicate shade he had ever seen. Short-lived whirlwinds of scarlet flame circled skyward as if hurled from the mouth of a massive cannon, only to burn themselves out and become lost in the gathering smoke. The entire forest seemed to be alight with weird,

glimmering sheets of light. Every few seconds
a rolling mass of gas would explode and light the
sky with green and lavender and old rose.
Through the slash it raged, its fiery wings out-
stretched, while here and there a great dead pine
burned at the top like a mammoth candle set in a
sea of foamy clouds.

He was gone again, down hill now, every muscle
responding to his will. In a few moments more
he swung wide the rustic gate, dashed up to the
porch and pounded fiercely on the cabin door.
Bob hastened to open it. Harry—hatless, coat-
less, stumbled in, crying, "Fire! Fire! Uncle,
the slash is a-fire! The mill, the lumber, the slabs
—the world is a-fire, burning, burning—" He
sank on the floor exhausted.

Bob gathered the lad in his arms and laid him
on the couch, as he called for Aunt Belle and
Tompkins. Soon a cool drink and a bit of water
dashed into his burning face brought him back.

"Why didn't you 'phone?" ordered Mr. Standish.

"Line's down," sobbed Harry. "Stack blew
over and snapped them off. Come, quick! They
need a leader out in the valley. Plenty of bosses
at camp, but nobody to direct the big fight. Come,
we must go."

Just then High put in his appearance, hobbling
in on his cane.

"High, do you suppose you could saddle up, while I get the Supervisor on the wire?—Yes, four horses. You better go with us, for you could carry orders. We will need every available man. Hear that gale, and Bald Knob Valley a-fire!"

"Hello—Bob—yes. Bald Knob's a-fire—mill, slash, lumber, all. Kable at Mountain City. Come, quick. Yes, every available man. Better telegraph for more men before you start. If the gale keeps up it will last a week. It means the entire valley a-fire by daylight unless the wind goes down. Plenty of dynamite at the mill. Yes, plenty of tools. Cabin safe unless wind changes."

Mr. Standish hurriedly got out three canteens from the corner, filled each with fresh water, stuffed a few first aid packets into his pocket, got gloves for High and Harry, and together they hastened out to the barn, High hobbling clumsily on his cane.

"Hitch up the spring wagon, Belle. Load all the cruise books, papers and provisions, and what else you think wise, and be ready to move. You are reasonably safe. Don't believe the fire can jump the fire balk on the ridge, but if she does, don't hesitate. We have talked it all out often enough for you to know what to do. I can trust you. Good-by!" And they were gone.

The gangs had gotten quickly into action as best they knew after the first few moments of surprise, and already the two force-pumps were pouring their tiny streams over the huge piles of freshly sawed lumber that stood in the clearing. The logging engine had gotten up steam, with the aid of a generous amount of oil, and was just preparing to run back into the deep woods. So far, the fire was all on the south of the track and an attempt would be made to keep it from jumping the track onto the other side. There were shovels, and rakes, and axes, and plenty of dynamite.

Every single man was alive to the real situation, and was a strange combination of the daredevil spirit of a seasoned woodsman balanced with absolute fearlessness and good judgment. If that old mill could ever be saved, it would be saved with such a gang of men if they just had a leader. The fight was on, yet how puny a few handfuls of men to fight such a monster!

Jaycox stood close to the side of the excited saw-master. His body was tense, his jaw set and determined. He must divert any possible suspicion from himself by fighting his best and by attracting attention to his efforts to save the mill. Evidently the saw-master believed his job was to stay by the mill and look out for the office and records, for suddenly he turned to Jaycox and ordered him to bury Kable's office effects, books, papers, money and all, safely and at once.

A few moments later, Mr. Standish, Tompkins,

High and the Scout dashed up to the mill and asked for the saw-master.

"Don't know how it started," he answered, in reply to the Ranger's first question. "It had great headway before we were awakened. You take charge, Standish, for this is an old game to you. We are all at your service.

"Might have been burned alive in that rat trap if this stack hadn't gone over. Don't know what struck it, perhaps lightning. It is evident she started well back at the end of the slash. It was either lightning, or friction, or—" he stopped short, "or some devil. She spread fast. She was one sheet of flame when I got out, yes, slash, slabs, and all."

Bob took in the situation almost at a glance, and was satisfied in his own mind at once that the fire had been set; yet he said nothing.

"High, go to the trail-head and await the Supervisor and his party," he said. "They ought to be here in less than an hour. Tell them I have the gangs all out, all organized and doing their best. The fight is to be on the log road and on north. I can see that much anyway. Tell him if things are not moving to suit him to send us orders. As long as you stay on Bess you are all right. She is seasoned to the core. She won't shy or fright, and will ride right into the flame if need be. Whatever you do, don't dismount.

You might lose her, and then you would be helpless with that crippled leg. Remember, stay
mounted.

"Scouts, you are to be the hospital. Here—"
and he emptied his pockets of first aid stuff. "It
won't be long until some one will be getting hurt.
Trees are beginning to fall. Be prepared. Get
water and a cot or two. Keep near the stream as
possible, and keep your eyes open. But mind
what I say, don't go into the burning area. If
you should get confused, you're lost. Watch the
wind and use your head."

He was off at a wild gallop, and was soon swallowed up in the dense smoke that the wind kept
blowing down the valley.

The boys had just completed their temporary
hospital and were going over to the office when
they met Jaycox coming out of it, his arms loaded
down with books and papers, preparatory to burying them for safety. He did not notice the boys at
first, but in hurrying on caught his foot on a stray
slab and fell sprawling. Letters and papers flew
in every direction and there was a wild scramble,
the Scouts helping to gather them in before the
wind got them. Jaycox held tight to the little
tin box in which Kable kept his money. Soon
they were packed in a box, dropped into a hastily
dug pit and a couple of feet of earth piled over
them. Jaycox then stuck his shovel in the ground

—"to mark the spot in case it would be hard to locate afterwards," he told the Scouts, but in reality the thought that was in his mind was to mark it so that he could come back for the money when all was over.

Under the direction of Mr. Standish the gangs toiled on. He was here, and there, and everywhere, giving his orders along the track. Backfires were set and gave promise of solving the problems. Three of the best teams were sent ahead to the north along a sandy ridge to plow a fire-balk in order to hem in the fire on the north. A big gang were already cutting a path to the west to try to keep the fire from the immense piles of logs that had not yet been moved to the mill. Dynamite was used extensively to blow up trees too big to stop to cut, while every effort was being made to reduce the fire from a top-fire to a ground-fire where it could be fought the better with fresh earth and hand tools.

Still the fiery avalanche swept on. The pall of smoke crept over the whole valley, and gas, that was now being generated in huge quantities, suffocated the men and reduced their effectiveness. Everywhere the wind was laden with sparks and shreds of burning bark. Once the main fire front crossed the slash area and got into the virgin timber it became a roaring hurricane of fire. The men were beaten back like insects and were com-

pelled to go to the next ridge and start all over
again. Many of them worked mechanically.
Their feet were blistered and their hands and
faces burned painfully, yet they toiled on doggedly, determinedly, to win.

Twice big raw-boned Jaycox came hurrying out
of the forest toward the boys with a collapsed
lumberman in his huge arms, deposited his load
at the makeshift hospital, and then disappeared
again, only to re-appear with a lifeless form. A
falling lodge pole had struck him full and he was
gone—killed doing his duty, with no one to applaud
his bravery.

The Scouts were filled with awe. Never before
in their lives had they felt so small or so insig-
nificant. Never before had they realized the awful power of Nature loosed in the wild. They
were destined to grow older that night and wiser
in many ways for boys.

As Jaycox deposited his dead burden, he said,
between great breaths, "There is another feller
badly hurt in yonder, but I must take orders to
Mr. Standish. You boys could get him. I'll
bring him to the edge. Make a litter. You can
carry him. It's little Jean, the cook."

There was no refusing such an appeal. They
must go, for Jean had been their best friend, and
anyway it was just to the edge of the timber.
Like lightning they had a stretcher made from a

light folding cot and were off following Jaycox, forgetting, for the instant, their orders from their Uncle Bob.

They had hardly disappeared in the dense smoke when the Supervisor, Tompkins, Toney, and a half dozen other men dashed into camp on heaving, panting horses. The Supervisor looked about eagerly for some one from whom he could get what information he needed. No one was in sight, and they were just about to take the North road when Jaycox came out of the smoke curtain and deposited another victim on the ground, apparently without noticing the new party.

"Where's Standish?" demanded Hastings. Jaycox waved his hand to take in the whole fire. "There," he said, "fighting."

"Where are the two boys, do you know?" demanded Toney, who had been thinking of them all the way over the ridge.

"Gone to get a dead Frenchman," growled Jaycox, impatient to be off. "They went over yonder a few minutes ago."

"In that sea of flame!—those boys?" demanded Toney, incredulously. "Did you tell them to go?"

Jaycox only shrugged his shoulders and turned to go, but Tompkins quickly reined in his horse and blocked him. His big Colt was held firmly in one hand. There was a determined gleam in his gray eyes. He had been thinking fast as he

rode to the fire that night, and had been turning
in his mind what the Sheriff had told him about
his visit to the saw mill a week before. He had
been wondering all the way over if Luke's boy
could be in that camp. He was positive of just
one thing: if he was there, it was he that lighted
that slash. The instant he saw Jaycox in that
weird half-light of burning trees he noted the
likeness. Almost instantly a train of ideas linked
themselves together in his mind and brought him
to a conviction.

"You are Old Luke's boy!" he shouted, fiercely.
"This fire is your work. Throw up your hands!
At last I have you!"

There was a snarl, like that of a wild animal at
bay, great billows of black smoke enveloped them,
and for a fleeting second all sight was blotted out.
Tompkins reached for his man. There was a sudden burst of red, a wild whirlwind of hungry
flame, and the end of the bunk-house blazed afire.

"See!" cried Jaycox. "There are the Scouts.
One is hurt." All hands turned to look. Jaycox
was gone. He dodged behind the slab pile, leaped
between the engine house and the kitchen, lay
down and rolled to the bunk-house, and was lost
from view. Tompkins fired three rapid shots,
but to no avail. Jaycox was gone. His clever
stall had saved his life, for the Scouts were no-
where in sight.

"That was the man who stole my gun from my cabin and brought me the bear meat," said Old High, excitedly.

"And who killed Jacobus!" said Tompkins, savagely. "And he has been in this mill, under our very noses, for two months. That Sheriff is a fool. Said he was here and couldn't find his man."

One of the injured men, who had been watching the whole scene, now spoke up. "Better hunt those boys, or you'll never see them again. They went yonder to get an injured man."

"High, see if you can locate them. Tell them to come out at once, no matter what they are at. Tompkins, skirt south with Toney and head off that desperado. He isn't armed this time, fortunately, and won't be to-night. Shoot on sight, shoot to kill. Forward, men, we will take the North road."

The little party split to obey orders. High rode into the heavy smoke, past piles of slash twenty feet high that had not as yet gotten a'fire. He worked his way toward the outskirts of the fire that was just dimly visible ahead. It was burning due north, that was plain to be seen, and it had already crossed the log road and was eating its way up the other slope. He could hear above the hiss of flame the occasional thud of exploding dynamite, and he knew full well just what was going on. They were working the north ridge of Bald Knob in an effort to keep the fire in the valley. Unless the wind changed, the mill and the lumber were going to be safe, but all else would be swept clear.

He stopped, and called and called. Once he thought he heard a faint reply. He followed it up, but the wind was so gusty and variable that he was not sure. His little mare quivered with excitement, and pawed the ground to be off. Suddenly a great pine that had been saturated with pitch and that stood near the edge of the fire exploded with a lurid glare and sent a pink flame high into the air. He caught just one glimpse of a youthful figure bending over a prostrate form. He urged Bess into the smoke and heat, and a moment later came to Harry kneeling over the form of his twin brother, sobbing and begging the lad to answer him. By their side lay the makeshift litter, and on it lay Jean, the camp cook, apparently dead.

Harry looked up at High, but so dazed was he that he failed to recognize him at all. High took in the situation at a glance. Harvey had been overcome with his burden and Harry would not leave him and could not carry him. The boy was sobbing out his heart, and begged High to take his brother and leave him to come on with Jean. High thought just a second. He had already made up his mind what to do in regard to himself, but how to save Jean, too, was the problem. He only too well realized that the instant he gave up his saddle, like as not he would be helpless; for, although his broken leg had healed after a fashion, he was a hopeless cripple and could not stand but a few steps without his crutch or a cane.

However, he slid out of the saddle, helped Harry mount, then leaning over he picked Harvey up with great effort and placed him in front of Harry, gave him careful direction, and told him to go as fast as he could, keep his brother in place, to dismount, get help, if possible, and to return with the horse for Jean and himself. Harry was off with him, of course, no thought but that he would get back at once to High and the body they had fought so valiantly to save from the Fire Fiend.

Three moments afterward the wind changed to straight down the valley. The hot ashes flew in showers, and everywhere little fires were starting. The heat was intense, the smoke was awful. Instantly High realized that his only chance lay in his being able to crawl to safety. He could not walk a dozen steps without his cane, he was certain. There was nothing else to do but to desert Jean. It was a matter of his own safety now. So he started forward. The fire was in the tops now, sixty feet above him. The wind was a gale: He struggled on and on, blindly, fiercely,—a man fighting the elements for his life. But Old High was not destined to win. He died fighting. He had given his life for his friends, and he was satisfied, for he knew that at last his name was clear of dishonor. Tompkins and the Scouts would take care of that.

They found his charred bones several days later, after a gushing rain had put a stop to the fire monster, pinioned beneath a great limb that had fallen on him from above as he endeavored to worm his way to safety.

All night long the men toiled and toiled, back-fired, plowed, and blasted, but every hour saw the hungry monster more powerful. The wind swept down the valley and defeated every plan. The bunk-house burned like a packing box. The mill went next, and then came the great pile of newly sawn lumber and ties. It was all swept clean to the black bare rock.

Tompkins had returned after a fruitless search for Jaycox, savage to think he had let the scoundrel get away alive. He found the boys in bad shape and the wounded men in danger of being burned alive. Alone and single-handed he moved them to a place of safety, Harry begging and entreating him all the while to go to High's rescue, but he had to refuse. There would be absolutely no use of risking his life also in that awful sea of flame.

"It would be wildest folly, lad. It would be simple suicide. We must just trust that High was able to save himself. If we never see him again, boys, we will know he died a brave man. If he does not return by daylight, we'll know he died the unselfish old man that I have always said he was.

"With the wind carrying clouds of deadly vapors on wings of fiery gales," continued Tompkins, "such as are now raging in yonder slash piles, no living thing could possibly survive it. I'd give my right arm for just one good shot at that fiend incarnate—Jaycox. I'm afraid I've bungled this game terribly."

"And our desperado is gone again!— And I've been talking to him every day! I knew it was he, but couldn't believe it. 'Courageous' recognized him and tried to tell us all, but we couldn't understand. Oh, what will Mr. Hastings say about this, anyway?" cried Harry.

"He'll simply storm when he knows the truth," said Tompkins, as he rode off again to do what he could with the fire.

The back-fire from the ridge crept slowly down till it met the oncoming flames. They met with a hiss, and in an hour the fire was safe from that quarter. At the end of the valley the back-fire had slipped control and was in danger of frustrating all they had accomplished on the ridge. On it come—a seething gale of flame, sweeping everything before it, wiping the ground clean as a new-swept floor except for the huge stumps here and there, that would stand to tell to the next generation of the awful devastations.

From the slab pile the fire had gotten into the next valley south, where stood the new virgin timber of the second tract that had not yet been touched beyond the cruising and marking. Down the valley it went, a roaring mass of flame-ridden trees that formed fiery pillars from the ground to their crowns, the heavens alight with the glare of burning tinder and dry bark, the air saturated with clouds of suffocating gas-capped smoke, the howl of the wind, the crash of falling trees, the oceans of living sparks that soared and flew ahead of the fire-front,—all made a scene that was enough to terrify the stoutest heart that ever fought a forest fire.

Then things changed. The gale died down. The first gray streaks of dawn could be seen in the east. The wind grew damp. First, came a gentle mist, then a fog, and finally a soft rain that increased until it became a downpour. Oh, what a relief to the tired, worn men on the ridges. What a sound of sizzling and snapping as the wet drops pelted the hot logs and stumps, turning instantly to steam.

A party had gone ahead, under the Supervisor's personal direction, to the mouth of the Famine

Valley, where they had carefully set a third back-fire, and by the time the rain was at its height the two columns of fire had met and were burning themselves out.

The valley was a graveyard with nothing left but thousands of blackened stubs and parched open spaces. The mill, the lumber, the slabs, all had vanished in a single night, and daylight found the most weary and most discouraged group of men the sun had ever shown upon. They had lost everything they owned, had whipped in a terrible fight, and, what was of far more consequence to them, they had lost work. In a single night a winter's steady employment had been snatched from their very hands. Their incomes had stopped. Work was slack, and there were women and kiddies that must be fed and clothed until spring.

They stood about the tiny stream talking matters over, as they bathed their tired feet and cooled their burned faces, and wished for their boss, Kable. They had been advised that he was on the way with money and wished to see them all. Twice Tompkins had been about to tell the crowd what he knew, but refrained him to keep still. No doubt he had reasons for the silence.

There were a thousand ideas expressed as to causes. There were a thousand minute explanations for the affair, but none were satisfactory. The men were carefully counted and checked into fire gangs, and all were accounted for but High Tucker, Jean, the French cook, and Jaycox.

When Harry, with streams of tears running down his face, told that weary, exhausted group of mountaineers the simple story of how High Tucker had given his own life for the Scouts there wasn't a dry eye in the crowd, and to a man they doffed their hats (those that had not lost them in the night) and gave a great shout for the grand old Prospector. Next came a shout for little Jean, the cook, that had died doing his duty. But when it came to a discussion of Jaycox there was a difference of opinion. Yet, when some one of the men that he had rescued from a fiery grave suggested a rah for him, too, Tompkins deftly diverted it by suggesting that there was no proof yet that he was dead, and that if they were going to laud living heroes, every man in the camp had one coming.

There was much gloom at the Standish cabin that day. Especially was Tompkins nervous and miserable, and every comment that he voiced showed how he blamed himself for letting Jaycox get away; but the truth had dawned upon him so quickly that he had not had time to think or plan. He was for organizing a posse at once, offering a reward for the scalawag, and going after Jaycox hard, but the Supervisor had ideas of his own and refused to grant permission.

In Harvey's pocket was found a letter sealed, but not addressed. All that he could remember was that he had picked it up after he saw Jaycox bury the office papers, and thinking it was one that had blown away he had put it in his pocket mechanically and had forgotten it until now.

The Supervisor opened it and read it, his face showing great surprise. He held it out to Tompkins with a shrug. "Read that, man. That desperado has a charmed life, I tell you."

The letter was written in Kable's hand and was to the Sheriff, telling him he believed he had at last discovered his man and asking him to come to the mill again under cover of night and together they would talk it out. In his hurry to get away to Mountain City the message had not been sent, and now, of course, it was too late. Jaycox was gone. But where?—That was the question that all wanted answered. Could it be possible that he, like High, had been burned,— burned in a fire of his own making. Tompkins was decidedly of the opinion not.

"We will never get him with a posse, Tompkins," said Mr. Hastings, positively, after some thought. "We have got to surprise the rascal. He can't get far, for he has no clothes, no mount, no food, no money, and—thank God, no gun this time. He is in these very hills in hiding. We must locate him at once, but it must be on the quiet. I wouldn't wonder he might be found at High's cabin at his hour, or at his mine. There are provisions there, and shelter, and he knows it."

"He had High's old rifle. What did he do with it?" said Uncle Bob.

"Oh, it probably burned with the bunk-house," replied the Supervisor.

"Now, let's get some rest and be ready by noon," said Hastings. "We'll make a close drag net and we'll hunt these hills night and day until we get that fiend. And when we once get him in that old calaboose—I—I was going to say we'd set it a'fire too; but, of course, we must let the law take its course. I know what a jury of these mill hands will do."

Aunt Belle prepared them a simple meal, while Uncle Bob got a report ready for the State Forester in Denver. Soon they were fast asleep, all save Tompkins, and he was eager to start.

Late that afternoon the Scouts journeyed back over the trail to the vast burned-over area to view it in its desolation. There was nothing left of their countless old "veterans" save gnarled and blackened stubs that rose on the hills by the hundred. They wandered here and there sadly—up the stream that was now full of floating débris and choked with half-burned limbs. They turned where the little stream swung about a great granite crag and were about to climb the mountain into the green living forest again, when Harry suddenly caught Harvey by the arm and pointed up stream.

There, with his nose deep in the cooling water, was "Courageous." But he had heard their approach, and with his sensitive nose tipped high to the wind he whiffed suspiciously, and was off into the near-by thicket.

"We'll hunt you to-morrow, old boy," said Harry, fervently, "and perhaps you and your gentle smeller can help us find Jaycox."

"I must bring my kodak and take some snaps of the awful ruin," said Harvey, "so we can tell the Scouts at home about it. It won't be many weeks now until we must go home."

"We'll have some yarns to tell, too, won't we?"

"Yes, but I'd rather catch that desperado than anything else in the world," said Harry. "I'd be a happy Scout if I could just do that. Perhaps it would in a measure pay for some of the awful blunders we have made, and for the death of High."

"Oh, I wish we could!" assented Harvey, eagerly, "but I'm afraid we never will. He's too clever."

"If we could only make sure he is still in the valley, the rest would be easy."

"But how can we?"

"I have a very faint idea, but I'm not ready to tell you yet. I must let it soak awhile first. Say, do you suppose there might have been any money in those papers from Mr. Kable's desk?— You know Jaycox buried them. If there was, and he knew it, he might come back, mightn't he, just to get it, after he is sure there is no one around to see him?"

"No one saw him bury those papers but we two boys," said Harvey, earnestly, "and perhaps he'll think we don't count. Do you suppose he will come back, old Scout?"

"I think he will, sometime," said Harry, "and then, watch me!"

Harvey waited for the details, but soon discovered they weren't forthcoming, at least just then, and soon they were on the trail again bound for the cabin.

CHAPTER X

"**I** WISH that posse would hurry and get back," said Harry, to his brother two days later. "We have got to stay pretty close until we see what they find out. It is my own candid opinion, though, that they won't get a trace of their man."

"What makes you think so, Scout?" queried Harvey. "Some of the best woodsmen in this part of the West are on his trail. I don't see how he can get away, unless some one shelters him."

"Yes, but you must remember he was born in the wild, he's lived in it all his life; in reality he is a wild animal. He has proven that a number of times. There are no doubt hundreds of wild things about us here this moment, but we never see them. They don't propose that we shall. I'll bet Jaycox could live right here for a long time without being caught, unless by accident."

"They may never hear of him again in these parts," said Harvey. "I think he's gone for good."

"I don't," said Harry, positively. "I think he

228

is in these very woods at this hour, for, unless I'm badly mistaken in our man, he will make at least one try to join his father and brothers before he makes his final get-away. I am determined to try my little stunt. If he *is* here, he'll come back to those buried papers, for you know he told us there was money there; but not while any one is watching him, of course. Probably he would come in the dead of night when he is least expected. Now, the surest way in the world to catch him is to first make certain he is still here, and I have an idea that's working.''

"Another pipe dream, I suppose,'' laughed Harvey. "How are you going to work it—lay over there in the brush until you hear a noise about that spot and then hurry out with a lantern and peer into his face to identify him? Better arrange to snap a cow bell about his neck quick, so you can follow him when he runs. Ha! Ha! old Scout, you are a great schemer, but you'll never get ahead of Jaycox.''

Harry was just a bit put out at the joking and his eager smile changed to determination. "I *was* going to tell you all about my little scheme, but now I wont,'' he said, decisively. "Not one word. And when I do catch my man, he shall be mine—do you hear? all mine!''

"Go to it, Scout, go to it! Here's luck a'plenty,'' laughed Harvey, lightly. Neverthe-

less, he was disappointed, for he always liked to
be in on Harry's schemes and down in his heart
he knew full well that they most always panned
out. He went into the cabin with just one thought
in his mind—getting some possible clew to Harry's
method.

"Those buried papers are the key," he said,
half aloud, "but I can't see how he's going to
catch him."

Harry walked over to the rustic gateway and
stood looking down the trail. Just over his head
ran the telephone wires, one set to the Supervisor's cabin down the valley, the other set over
the ridge to the scene of the great fire only two
days before. The boy was lost in thought. He
was busy adjusting the conditions to his embryo
scheme, but it was very evident there were some
fundamentals lacking that he was at a loss to
know just how to supply. At last he knelt down,
picked up a bit of a stick and began to visualize
his idea on the ground with a crude sketch. He
became so engrossed that he began talking aloud,
as if explaining to a close companion.

"You see, old boy," he was saying, "I've got
to do three big things: I've got to prove that
some one really tampers with those papers and
that money, that that some one is Jaycox, and I
have got to be advised of his visit the instant he
begins to dig. Now, those are three real corkers.

No doubt, if he does come, he'll come in the night; at least, that's my only chance. But if he should reconnoiter before dark to see if all's well, he'll see my kodak and that would be the end of it all. Now if I try to hide it he will be sure to notice the change of things. The other thing that simply sticks me is how in Sam Patch am I to get current enough over there to set off that flashlight. Wish to goodness I had one of my old storage batteries here. I can arrange the opening and closing of the shutter easily. That came to me in the night.

"I wish Harvey hadn't shown that spirit. I'll need him to help, but I won't tell him—not a word now. He can wait. Let's see, that posse ought to be home at least by to-morrow night. If they haven't gotten him and he is still at large he is very liable to take a look at those papers to-morrow night. Say, boys, I've got to dust and get my machine ready. There is no time to lose. What's the good of a bright idea if it's too late, I'd like to know?"

He broke into a merry laugh as he thought how surprised they would all be if he *should* do the trick. "Be some glory to just hand the Supervisor a portrait of old Jaycox digging that hole, after the best posse in the West declares he's gone! I hope they haven't had any luck."

He slipped into the cabin, emptied his duffle bag

and swung it to his shoulder. Then when no one was looking he slipped his kodak, tripod, and a new package of flash cartridges into it and made a bee line for the little shop at the end of the wood-shed. Once in, he shut the door softly—he was sure no one had seen him enter—and began to look for needful accessories.

Yes, there was copper wire, and a hinge, and a piece of two-by-four that would be just the thing. Yes, what was more, there were two hinges and one of them was brass. That settled another try-ing problem. He knew there must be dry cells there somewhere, for his uncle used them both for the 'phone and for his electric lanterns in the barns.

To his delight he found a new box of a dozen batteries that had just come. In fact, they had not been opened yet. He would remove what he needed and replace the lid so they would never be missed, at least for the present. If he was just successful, then he would tell them all about it, but if it was a failure he would just return them to their place and no one would be any the wiser.

He sawed the two-by-four into two pieces about twenty inches long. These he hinged together at one end so they would fold up easily like a letter U. Next he took the brass hinge apart by pull-ing out the pin and mounted one-half on the in-side end of each stick, so that when the two-by-four was folded up tight the two parts of brass would fit into each other, like an electric switch. He adjusted these carefully so as to insure a perfect electrical contact for his wires. He then loosened one screw sufficiently from each half of the hinge so as to fasten the end of a small copper wire to each screw-head. He again tightened them up and quickly attached the other ends of the wires to one of the batteries. Then he opened and shut the huge switch. To his great delight, the instant the two brass pieces would come in contact with each other there was a sharp spark. He added a second battery, and then a third and fourth, until he was entirely satisfied that there was enough spark to set off the flash powder.

Next he constructed a careful coil of copper wires about one-half inch in length and made it fast to one of the brass hinge parts so as to stand erect against the other.

"You see," he was saying, "I must allow for the depth of the powder between the two and must be sure of my contact." He tried the improved contact, but it failed to suit him, so he removed the coil and simply attached to each side of the hinge a small wire that he could lead off to his powder cartridge a bit at one side. This worked better, and he was satisfied.

"But how in Sam Hill am I to squeeze that bulb sharp enough to be sure of an exposure?" He stood looking at his machine, when suddenly another bright idea flashed into his mind. He winked knowingly, as if to an observing companion, and then put his idea into practice.

He placed the bulb of his kodak at the exact point of the hinged joint, wired it there with a bit of a wire, and then lifting the one end of the hinged two-by-four he let it drop quickly, so as to pinch the bulb suddenly. It was heavy enough to flatten the bulb to quite a degree, but not enough to completely force out the air. In a moment that was arranged by securely fastening a brick at the end of the top half of the pincher. It worked like a charm, and what was more to be thankful for, it insured a splendid contact for his current. Every time he tried it he discovered that the bulb was just enough nearer so that the kodak shutter completely opened just a flash before the spark took place.

"Couldn't be better!" he exclaimed, enthusiastically, and then his face fell. "But how am I going to cock the thing and shoot it? Say, it will take a post-graduate of Boston Tech to run this thing yet. Bone-head!" he cried, suddenly. "That's the easiest of all. I'll just prop these two pieces of two-by-four apart with a light bit of limb, tie a stout string—a fish line is just the wrinkle—to the prop, and the other end I'll fasten in the earth just where the papers are, say to a bit of wood. He's just naturally bound to throw that chip out as he digs, and when he does, pop will go the weasel!—out comes the prop, bing goes the bulb, puff goes the flash light, and quicker than scat Mr. Jaycox will have his beauty struck. Great! But—" The Scout's face fell. "Say, what if he should take a notion to investigate? He would find my kodak sure, and go away with it, and then what? Oh, fiddle! there goes another bright idea all to smash." His face fell as he stopped to survey his work.

"If there was just some way of getting a signal back to the cabin that the thing had happened, or even back into the woods, say three or four hundred yards, so we could close in on him! I'd almost be willing to lose my kodak if I could only catch the desperado." He was lost in thought, but try as he might he could get no solution.

"Don't know just how I could hide the thing, either," he said, at length, quite disgustedly. "I'm glad I didn't tell Harvey about it now, 'cause it looks like it's all up. Too bad, too!"

He carefully put all his parts out of sight in his duffle bag and slipped out around the barn. Forcing a whistle to his lips, he opened the door and went into the cabin.

Harvey was reading a letter and was completely absorbed.

"Who's the letter from, Scout?"

Harvey scowled a bit and tossed it over to Harry.

"From Mother; and she thinks we better plan to come home before Christmas. Scarlet fever is better and they are getting lonesome for us."

Harry read the letter eagerly, then turning to his brother he haid, half bitterly:

"I wouldn't mind going half so much if we could just get Jaycox first."

"Well, I thought you said you *were* going to get him," challenged his brother. "Won't that infernal machine you have been working on do the trick?" There was just a bit of triumph in his voice.

Harry looked at him angrily. "How did you know? Have you been spying on me?"

"Of course not. I'm a Scout, and Scouts play fair," retorted Harvey. "I was just guessing."

"Well, I had an idea, but it won't work," said Harry despondently. "I was in hopes it would, but it won't."

The telephone rang vigorously. Harry hurried to the receiver. "Yes, Harry Carter. You, Tompkins? Didn't catch him; no signs. Well, well. Not at High's cabin or hadn't been there. Well, what you going to do now?— Coming here to-night to do a little investigating on your own hook; think he is here somewhere. Do you really think so? Say, Tompkins, listen!" said Harry eagerly. "I want to see you just as soon as you get here, private like. No, I don't know anything for sure, but I have an idea. Perhaps you and I could— You'll be here at four? I'll be ready for you. Say, is there such a thing as a small electric bell there at headquarters? There is? Well, hurray! Bring it with you without fail. Goodby."

"Now for work," said Harry. "Scout, I'm going to take you in on this deal after all, because I've had a new inspiration and I tell you my little scheme is going to work. If we catch that desperado it would be too bad for you not to have had a hand."

Together they went to the shop, and Harry carefully explained and then demonstrated his idea.

"Great!" shouted Harvey. "Scout, you are a regular wonder. But what are you going to do with the bell?"

"Simple," replied Harry. "Listen. I was lost completely till I heard that 'phone ring. Suddenly I thought of the down telephone wires from the mill. We'll hook the bell on this end and into the circuit, use the power that is on the line already for transmission and spark, and the instant there is contact the bell will ring here in this cabin. See? Now all that means is to find some way to hide the outfit over at the mill. That's what is bothering me most just now."

"Oh, that's easy!" cried Harvey, now fully enthused over the plan. "Why not put your whole machine inside the big boiler? You know the open end looks exactly out on the spot where the papers are buried; and say, Scout, those wires will just about reach to it. I mean the loose ends from the bunk-house."

"You've got it, old boy!" cried Harry excitedly. "Two heads are better than one any day. Scout, I'm glad I took you in."

They watched eagerly for the home-coming of Uncle Bob, Toney, Tompkins and the Supervisor, and sure enough it was just four-thirty when they rode up the trail, tired and hungry and on horses that were nearly exhausted. The boys knew at a glance that they had ridden hard and long, and asked no questions. It was very plain to be seen that the Supervisor was completely out of sorts.

An early supper over, Tompkins and the two Scouts excused themselves, and the Government Ranger was introduced to the intricacies of the new automatic detective. He listened patiently as Harry explained, but instead of catching the enthusiasm of the boys, Tompkins' brow clouded and his tired face frowned in spite of himself. At last he interrupted:

"Scouts, that's a very ingenious idea that you have there, no doubt, but you boys are all wrong. You don't realize how tremendously important it

is to this whole State that we catch that scalawag.
It's not the job of boys, even if they are Scouts,
to undertake to capture desperate criminals
merely in order to prove they are clever boys.
The thing to do always is to get any information
you may have into the hands of the proper civil
authorities at once. The Supervisor must not
know, if we can help it, that you boys kept back
this information about the papers and the money.
That is the most important clew we have. I doubt
if we would have gone on that long, weary chase
to-day if we had known what you have now told
me.''

"But we'll catch him yet," said Harry, "and
that will make up for our thoughtlessness. Oh,
I'm so sorry I didn't think of it that way before.
I thought I was doing what was best."

"Anyway," said Tompkins, "the kodak part of
your scheme is all useless. We don't need a photograph of Jaycox. All we need to know is that
a man comes to those buried papers. Now, look
here, boys, don't be so glum. You may be the
means of capturing that crook yet. Listen! Instead of fixing the kodak as you suggest, we'll run
the wires into the old boiler and then we'll put the
bell back in the thick timber on the end of the line.
One of you boys will hide in the boiler and when
Jaycox comes, if he does, you signal the rest of
us by the bell and we'll quietly close in on him

from all sides while he digs, making his capture certain. He will never think to look inside that boiler even if he does reconnoiter the place and we'll get word the minute he begins to dig. What say you?" and he slapped the boys on the back to cheer them up.

They were both disappointed at the turn of affairs, but were perfectly willing to follow any suggestion Tompkins might make because of their confidence in him. In thirty minutes they were off in the woods with the necessary paraphernalia. The bell was attached to the telephone wires and run down a tree in a big sheltered ravine where they would be out of the wind and very near to the mill.

After talking the new plan over carefully it was decided to leave the kodak out of the consideration entirely and Harvey was to be the Scout that was to hide inside the boiler and give the alarm. They hurried off to make the proper connections and then back to talk it out with Uncle Bob and Toney before dark, for it would take them all to make the capture certain.

They were too tired to receive even this new clew with any real enthusiasm, but as Tompkins pointed out the possibilities in it, they finally warmed to the idea and soon were making final arrangements for the experiment. Every detail was carefully gone over and at last Harry in com-

pany with Toney, for Mr. Standish did not wish
to risk the unprotected boy there alone, set off for
the old boiler. It was decidedly a tight fit for
them and necessitated a very cramped position for
them both, but this was forgotten in the excitement of the thing.

"If we only do catch him!" breathed Harry to
his tired comrade.

"I hope we shall, my boy," said Toney, "but
whatever happens don't leave the boiler till I tell
you. I am responsible for you."

Harry promised and soon all was in readiness.
The last long rays of sunshine were shooting over
the western ridge of the fire-burned area, its red
glare in the burned timber strangely reminding
the Scout of that other night, the effects of which
he had not as yet completely gotten over.

In a few moments more Harvey, Mr. Standish
and Tompkins were safe in their retreat. Tompkins had his powerful pocket flash lamp with him
that sent a long, straight beam of yellow light far
into the night, and Uncle Bob his rifle ready for
any emergency. As they were all very weary,
Tompkins decided it was useless for all of them to
stay awake, so he volunteered to keep watch while
the others slept.

He found it hard to keep his eyes open, but so
eager was he to catch Jaycox that he was able to
keep the sleep from his eyes for hours. At nine

o'clock he felt compelled to walk back and forth to keep from dozing off, and when ten o'clock rolled around the ridiculousness of the thing began to dawn upon him, and he became so weary that he felt sure he could not stay awake another hour. Finally he sat down on an old stump to rest and look at the stars, and before he realized it he was sound asleep.

For an hour they slept on in peaceful slumber, and then Harry awakened. He called softly, and there was no reply. He rose hurriedly and looked about him, fearing Tompkins had heard something and had gone and left them while he reconnoitered. In a second, however, he found Tompkins fast asleep, and realized for the first time how utterly weary and worn the man was. He took his place by his side and waited. Surely minutes never passed so slowly before. Twice he caught himself nodding, and the same thoughts flashed through his mind that had come to the Ranger just before he had fallen asleep. Ten minutes more and Harry Carter would have been asleep alongside of the Ranger, but luck smiled upon him and saved him from what would have been the biggest defeat of his life.

The bell purred for a fleeting second, so softly that at first he believed he was dreaming, and then suddenly there were half a dozen vibrations; then all was still. Strange prickly chills ran up and down his spine. He shook Tompkins violently. The Ranger was alert in a second.

"The bell rang!" said Harry breathlessly.

"And I was asleep!" said Tompkins reproach- fully. "This way." They hurried forward over the trail. They had been in the absolute darkness all evening and were able to see surprisingly well.

When within a hundred yards they stopped short, Tompkins with his light ready to flash and Uncle Bob with his rifle ready for action.

"I hear him digging!" said Uncle Bob hoarsely.

"So do I," added Harvey in great excitement.

"He's there all right," breathed Tompkins. "I'll flash the light on him and you cover him, Bob. If he runs, shoot, but look out for the boiler. Let's not turn this chase into a tragedy for our- selves."

The light was flashed in the direction of the dig- ging. Tompkins heard a curse as he cried, "Hands up or you're a dead man!" Before them, outlined against the blackest of stumps, was a huge man, tattered and torn, his shoulders bent, and in his hands he clasped an ancient rifle. He stood staring into the blinding beam of light a second as if uncertain, and then leaped into the dark like an arrow, but not before Uncle Bob had fired. He heard the retreating figure fall. Toney hurried forward now, covering the prostrate form from behind. Fifty feet from where the beam had first outlined him lay Jaycox, shot in the leg,—a writhing, cursing mass of humanity. He was quickly disarmed and leaned against a stump. Toney called to Harvey to come on and soon they stood in an excited circle about their desperado. Soon he was bound as his father had been before him and a start was made for the cabin.

It was an interesting procession of Rangers, Scouts and horses that reached the cabin barnyard just before midnight. All were too tired to talk much, yet in the heart of each was a genuine satisfaction.

"We'll sure have some great experiences to tell the troop about, won't we?" said Harry enthusiastically.

"We sure will that," said Harvey, "from trout fishing to helping capture desperate tie cutters. My! but they will be interested in it all."

"I haven't had time to write in my diary, either," said Harry, "but I guess I can remember most of what I would have written."

"Oh, yes," laughed Harvey, "and some things that you wouldn't have written, too. Say, I'll have a great joke on you when I get to telling of how you planned to catch a desperado with a kodak!"

"If you tell that, Old Scout," laughed Harry, shaking his fist, "I'll thrash you for once good and proper."

"We'll see about that," retorted Harvey. "My muscles are awfully powerful just now. This forest life has put pep into me for sure."

"But what's to be done with this desperado," asked Harry eagerly, "now that we really have him?"

"We are going to keep him here until arrangements can be made to get him safely to the Mountain City jail. It would never do to lock him up here and let it be known, for those mill hands would have a picnic."

Early the next day Tompkins rode to Mountain City to bring Kable, and after a few hours with the miserable Jaycox they were entirely satisfied that they at last had the most sought-after man in the Famine Valley region.

The boys waited eagerly for the results of the talk, and when Tompkins told them that Jaycox had been living in a shanty in the burned-over area, they were anxious to see it; so following what general directions they could get they started to locate the hiding place.

By noon they found it—as clever a ruse as ever could be arranged. It was built of burned logs stood on end in a half circle about a huge standing stub, with a lot of smaller burned stuff scattered over the outside to destroy the appearance of regularity. Inside, to their utter astonishment, was a sharp ax, a saw, quite a lot of canned goods,

and an old water pail.   Far back in the corner was
a crude bed of boughs that had been brought from
the ridge in the dead of night.   Carefully Harry
photographed it from every angle, and then hurried home to develop them.

"Well, we helped to get him after all, Old
Scout!" said Harry, with real satisfaction.

"You bet we did," replied Harvey, "and now I
am ready to go home for Christmas."

That night there came a second letter from
home urging the lads to come as soon as convenient.   And so it was planned that they should go
to the State Forest Nursery for a few days, then
on to Denver, and from there leave for the East.

"We'll miss you very much, boys," said Uncle
Bob, "but we'll hope to have you back again in a
few years."

"We'll both be here, Uncle," cried Harry, "for
we have had the time of our lives.   You must be
sure to let us know what the law does with *our*
desperado, and, remember, we want to be foresters
ourselves one of these days."

THE END

THE BOY SCOUT LIFE SERIES

Published with the approval of
The Boy Scouts of America

In the boys' world of story books, none better than those about boy scouts arrest and grip attention. In a most alluring way, the stories in the BOY SCOUT LIFE SERIES tell of the glorious good times and wonderful adventures of boy scouts.

All the books were written by authors possessed of an intimate knowledge of this greatest of all movements organized for the welfare of boys, and are published with the approval of the National Headquarters of the Boy Scouts of America.

The Chief Scout Librarian, Mr. F. K. Mathiews, writes concerning them: "It is a bully bunch of books. I hope you will sell 100,000 copies of each one, for these stories are the sort that will help instead of hurt our movement."

Publishers
BARSE & CO.

New York, N. Y.   Newark, N. J.

THE MERRY MEN OF ROBIN HOOD PATROL

By

CHARLES H. LERRIGO

For boys from 10 to 16.

NET $1.50

WHEN Robin Hood Patrol started "out west" in search of the missing "Lord Pop" it numbered only four scouts, a Patrol Leader, and Peppermint. Mint was the dog. He was only vest-pocket size, but Wow! what a noise he could raise as a watchdog! Bill Frisk, who came from "out where the west begins," practically gave the Patrol the Royal 8, which turned out to be the best touring car ever made. The scouts go thru fire and water, not to mention a volcano, before they finally locate the Gold Mine of Robin Hood Patrol. And if they had not been guided by Da Na Yazzi, the Navajo, and if Bill Frisk had not been an ex-sheriff of Nye County who knew when to take up a gun and when to leave it alone, perhaps the Duke gang—you had better read the story.

———

PUBLISHERS

BARSE & CO.

NEW YORK, N. Y.   NEWARK, N. J.

THE BIG WAR SERIES

By

ROSS KAY

For Boys from 12 to 16

CLOTH   **12 MO.**   **ILLUSTRATED**

THE action of these thrilling stories takes place against the grim background of the huge European War.

This series does not contain lengthy studies of campaigns which would prove tiresome to the younger generation, but is packed with swiftly moving events. Authentic, instructive, and exciting, these stories of boys' adventures in the Great War are among our best and most popular series. Read one and you'll read the rest.

1. **THE SEARCH FOR THE SPY.**
2. **THE AIR SCOUT.**
3. **DODGING THE NORTH SEA MINES.**
4. **WITH JOFFRE ON THE BATTLE LINE.**

Publishers

BARSE & CO.

New York, N. Y.   Newark, N. J.

The Camp Fire Boys Series

By OLIVER LEE CLIFTON

For Boys from 8 to 14

A group of resourceful boys living in a small town form a camping and hiking club, which brings them all sorts of outdoor adventures. In the first story, "At Log Cabin Bend," they solve a series of mysteries but not until after some lively thrills which will cause other boys to sit on the edge of their chairs. The next story telling of their search for a lost army aviator in "Muskrat Swamp" is just as lively. The boys are all likable and manly—just the sort of fellows that every other wide-awake boy would be glad to go hiking with.

THE CAMP FIRE BOYS AT LOG CABIN BEND

THE CAMP FIRE BOYS IN MUSKRAT SWAMP

THE CAMP FIRE BOYS AT SILVER FOX FARM

THE CAMP FIRE BOYS' CANOE CRUISE.

THE CAMP FIRE BOYS' TRACKING SQUAD

———

PUBLISHERS
BARSE & CO.
NEW YORK, N. Y.   NEWARK, N. J.